Constructing Dalit Theology
for Dalit Liberation

Constructing Dalit Theology
for Dalit Liberation

J. A. David Onesimu

2012

Constructing Dalit Theology for Dalit Liberation — Published by the Rev. Dr. Ashish Amos of Indian Society for Promoting Christian Knowledge (ISPCK), Post Box 1585, 1654 Madarsa Road, Kashmere Gate, Delhi-110006.

© Author, 2012

ISBN: 978-81-8465-234-5

Laser typeset by **ISPCK,** Post Box 1585,
1654 Madarsa Road, Kashmere Gate, Delhi-110006
Tel: 23866322, 23866323
e-mail–ashish@ispck.org.in   • ella@ispck.org.in
website-www.ispck.org.

*This book is dedicated with special remembrance to
my parents, Late Rev. D. John Albert and
Dorothy Kovilammal, and to my brothers,
Late Mr. David Livingston and Rev Jeyasing Samuel.*

Contents

Foreword

I am delighted to write the foreword to this book written by Rev. Dr. David Onesimu, Principal, MTSC, and one of the senior pastors of Evangelical Church of India. I am glad that his dissertation for the Doctor of Philosophy degree, *Constructing Dalit Theology for the Liberation of the Dalit People*, is now available in the form of a book. This theological study is meant to enlighten the Christians in Indian churches who still practise the despicable caste system, consciously or unconsciously.

"Dalit", in general, refers to the much neglected people who are oppressed by the socially and economically powerful upper classes of India. I strongly believe that there is no place for such oppression in a God-fearing society. Particularly, there should not be any kind of encouragement to this evil in the churches. The God of the Bible is against oppressors. As the Psalmist points out, "The Lord executes righteousness and justice for all who are oppressed" (Ps.103:6). Therefore, as God's people, Christians can never oppress their own brethren, either in the church or in society.

The word "dalit" has its biblical origins in the Book of Exodus, which describes the cruel practice of slavery and oppression of the Israelites by the Egyptian Pharaohs for more than four centuries. (The word *dalit* is derived from the Semitic Hebrew root-word *dal*, which means "to crush" or "to be trodden down"). The Dalits of India have been under the worst kind of slavery and oppression by the Aryans, who came from Central Asia about two thousand years ago. They introduced their Vedic religion and the "Varnashra Dharm" – a four-tier caste system – among the Dravidian people who were the original inhabitants of the Indian Subcontinent. Archaeological findings prove that the Dravidians of the Sindh Valley Civilisation were a progressive and cultured people and, as such, they would have never practised this kind of an evil caste system.

Now, after the intrusion of the Aryans, the people and their culture have been affected to such an extent that, as the author points out, the dalits are not given any status in the four-layered caste system and are treated as "untouchables." This was the evil design of the Aryans to suppress the Dalits, the descendants of the original enlightened Dravidians of the Sindh Valley Civilisation.

The author has made an in-depth study of the liberation theologies of many other nations in the Orient, especially Korea, which produced the Korean Minjung Theology — the theology that exposes the condition of the suppressed people of Korea. In the Bible, as the early prophets pointed out, the answer to any kind of oppression was found in the coming of the Messiah. As the prophet Isaiah predicted, in the advent of the Messiah, Lord Jesus Christ, lies the answer to this social, economical and religious oppression (Is.61:1-3; Luke 4:17-20).

I appreciate the writer's hard work and sincere efforts to present Dalit Theology as the right remedy for the evil practice of caste prevalent among the present-day Christians in India. I am confident that this book will open the eyes of the Christians and urge them to strive for the removal of this great hurdle in presenting the Gospel and the planting of churches among the downtrodden people who, as we know, comprise a majority of the Indian population. I am quite confident that this research in Dalit Theology will benefit hundreds of researchers in the days to come in India and in the other nations of the East and the West.

Bishop Ezra Sargunam
Bishop-President
Evangelical Church of India

N

In his scholarly work, Rev. Dr. J. A. David Onesimu has meticulously examined how the ancient Hindu society organised along the caste system has the religious sanction of Brahmanical Hinduism. The caste system is based on the principle of discrimination and inequality and is one of the most rigid and  institutionalised brutalities of the Hindu society. Brahaminism uses the ideology of caste as a crucial instrument to dehumanise, divide and dominate the lower castes, Dalits in particular. Different caste groups are separated from each other in matters of marriage, physical contact and food by rules of purity and pollution. The entire worth depends on the position one occupies on the hierarchical scale of caste. In Hinduism, identity depends upon worth, and worth is determined as people are born and reborn in accordance with their *karmas*. This certainly breaks down harmony of relationships and perpetuates dehumanising oppression. Vengal Chakkarai, a high-caste Hindu convert to Christ, advocated that the church should "confront Hinduism on the plains of life." By this, he meant confronting caste oppression and exploitation. Economic projects as such do not help poor people to develop the crucial sense of self-worth. Rather, self-worth is the foundation for human growth and dignity. The gospel transforms the perception of the Dalits from worthless failures to an appreciation that in Christ they have the same worth as all other people. The Church helped Nadar women gain the right to cover their upper bodies during the violent breast-cloth controversy of the early to mid nineteenth century. Nadar women were frequently attacked, stripped and beaten and chapels and schools were burned for the offence of wearing the breast cloths previously worn by higher-caste Nair women. Empowered by the gospel of Jesus Christ, Nadars became leaders in the movement for social change.

Dr. Onesimu has clearly portrayed the prevailing caste thinking in many Church denominations of India. His emphasis needs to be noted that "any attempt at Dalit Theology will have to pay attention to the Dalit reality as a whole—with its historical, cultural, social, economic, political, theological and artistic aspects." While the agenda for political freedom of India from British rule was achieved in 1947, the freedom to emancipate the masses from perpetual exploitation and oppression remains to be won.

The Crucified God shares the pain of the Dalits and God in Jesus Christ provides the needed healing and courage to engage in issues of justice for all. The church in mission must bring the gospel of human dignity in Jesus Christ and create just and reconciled communities. We are called to live the gospel of Christ in oppressive structures of Indian society. The book invites the reader to engage with its context and develop a praxis for mission.

Rev. Dr. Richard Howell
General Secretary
Evangelical Fellowship of India &
Asia Evangelical Alliance

Acknowledgements

This is God's doing, it is wonderful in my sight. I thank God for His wonderful grace of salvation and for the miraculous ways of guidance in the vocation of serving Him. This is beyond my dream and happened because of God's predestined plan. I am thankful to God Almighty for all His blessings and for being my mentor and guide.

I am specially grateful to Asia United Theological University-ACTS for making this project a success. Thanks are due to President Dr. Lim Taek-Kwon, the then President of ACTS and Dr. Se Jin Koh, the Presiding President of ACTS. I am also grateful to our ECI Bishop President Most Rev. Dr Ezra Sargunam for his permission to do my research work with this institution. Also, I am thankful to our ECI Chennai Bishop Rt. Rev. Dr. Sundarsingh for his encouragement and valuable suggestion for this study. I am so thankful to the donor church of my scholarship through the Asian Centre for Theological Studies and Mission and Rev. Dr. Im Ik Kwon, Senior Pastor, Sae Han Presbyterian Church, Korea, for granting full scholarship for my studies in Korea. I am grateful to the president, faculty and staffs of this prestigious university for their love and care for me.

This work was accomplished with the constant encouragement, support and guidance of my advisor Dr. Han Sang Hwa (Ph.D., West Minister, USA), the precious daughter of the great theologian Dr. Han Chul Ha, the founder and first President of ACTS, and the readers Dr. Chung, Hong-Yul (Doctorate, Theology, Tubingen University, Germany) and Dr. Prof. Park, Hae- Kyung (Ph.D., Trinity International University, Chicago). I am also thankful to Dr. George Edward and. Mrs. Rebecca Azariah for editing this work.

In addition, I am thankful to all international students and Korean students of this university for their fellowship and love for me. I am so grateful to God for His wonderful people—those who have deeply influenced my life and ministry: Rev. Lee Man Shin and Rev. Han kee Chae of the Central Evangelical Holiness Church, Rev. Lee Sang Tae of Seo Kwang Evangelical Holiness Church and Rev. Han Hong Shick of the Jireh Holiness Evangelical Church.

I will always be grateful to my wife Epsi Beula and my beloved son Ezra Leander Santhosh for their love and affection for me and for showing a lot of patience during my research in Korea. My special thanks go to my parents-in-law, Mrs. and Mr. Job Kannappa, my brothers and sisters and their families for their prayers and support. I specially acknowledge the influences and support of Dr. S. J. Kingsly, Chairman, MTSC Board, and all other faculty members. I am also grateful to Ms. Sarala Sudamani for typing the first draft of this book.

Preface

This book aims to construct Dalit Theology for the liberation of the Dalit people, particularly Christian Dalits. The introduction to the book introduces the Indian society — a society dominated by the evils of the caste system. The Christian Church in her existence in a Hindu environment has adopted the caste system and is practicing caste in her structures and among her believers. So there is an urgency to recover our tradition of faith and to permit that tradition to permeate our Christian vocation. In this book, the author tries to recover the biblical vision and construct Dalit Theology exclusively for the Dalits in order to orient the reader towards authentic Christian discipleship, thereby challenging him or her to work towards the dismantling of the caste system that undergirds and makes possible an oppressive culture.

The caste system in India dominates interpersonal and inter-group relations. So, the first chapter gives an analysis of the caste system, tracing its origin from the ancient time, when the seeds of discrimination were sowed among the native people. It also focuses on the reform and social movements for eliminating the caste system in India.

The second chapter gives an insight into the history of the Dalits as the fifth caste, bringing in the study of their origin and their positions in different religions. It also focuses on the sociological factors that make the Dalits a "NO" community and deny them access to various basic services. It also presents the reality of the Dalits in history and contemporary times supported by archeological and literary evidences. In addition, the chapter gives a description of the life of the Dalits, including their religion, real-life condition, society, house and women. It also includes the responses of leaders such as Mahatma Gandhi, B. R. Ambedkar and E. V. Ramaswamy Naicker and the Church to the cause of Dalit Liberation.

The third chapter makes a study of similar types of theologies, such as Traditional Western Theology, Third World Liberation Theology, Latin American Liberation Theology, Water Buffalo Theology, EATWOT Theology and Korean Minjung Theology—theologies that have taken shape from the pains, struggles and oppression of the common people. Based on this study and an understanding of Indian Christian Theology, the chapter gives valuable insights into developing Dalit Theology.

The fourth chapter attempts to construct Dalit Theology, which surveys the situation of the suffering people by caste division and tries to bring a new ideology for Dalit Liberation. This includes the study of process, content, background and biblical paradigms. The chapter also considers Bible as a source for Dalit Theology, with an emphasis on Dalit Pathos from the biblical perspective.

The fifth chapter draws some lessons for constructing Dalit Theology and its implications for the liberation of Dalit people in India. This brings out Dalit consciousness, which is understood by Dalit liberation theologians through its nature, scope and purpose. It also brings out the theological reflection seeking the meaning of the present in the light of the history of God's redemptive acts and purposes. Theology and mission are inseparable and a truly contextual Dalit theology is one that empowers the Dalit church in mission involving a study of a Dalit God and Jesus the Dalit, the Christian contribution to Dalit Liberation highlighting the role of conversion, the never-ending caste war, the role of Christians, the Dalits betrayed and the need for change in the attitude of the church. This understanding takes the reader to a Dalit Liberative Hermeneutics, emphasising the roots of Dalit Liberation by enhancing the process by following important methodological observations and analysing Dalit Theology as a tool for future direction for the liberation of the Dalits.

The conclusion to the book supports the view that the Dalits have the right to life and that there is no reason why they should not live life to the fullest. In addition, it brings to light the Dalit God who shares the pathos of the Dalit people and provides the healing they need to carry on their struggle and realise their full humanity; it also calls the Church to rethink mission in the context of the Dalits and reformulate her message to be relevant and meaningful to the Dalits.

I thank all those who supported my research, and I especially thank Overseas Council Australia for their generous fund and ISPCK, Delhi, for publishing this book.

List of Abbreviations

ACTS.,	Asian Center for Theological Studies
ed.,	edition; edited by; editor (plural, eds.)
Ibid., *ibidem,*	In the same place
KETS.,	Korean Evangelical Theological Society
n.d.,	no date
n.p.,	no place, no publisher
Vol.,	Volume (plural, vols.)
WCC	World Council of Churches
Hindus	A Religion in India
Varna System	Dividing people on the basis of coloring
Savarnas,	Those with favorable color/ higher castes
Avarnas	Excluded or exterior groups
Dalit Jagruthi Samithi,	Dalits universal society
Harijans.	It is a given title for Dalits by Narsi Mehta in1920 at Gujarat
varnashrama,	Color based duty/work
shudras	Fourth lower class among the high Caste Hindus
vaishyas;	Third lower class among the high Caste Hindus
kshatriyas;	*Rajanya* is the other name for the second lower class among the high Caste Hindus

brahmanas	The first class among the high Caste Hindus
Purusa Sukta	A Slogan with in the Rig Veda
Sruti	The primary form of Hindu Scripture is called Sruti. It is what pioneers of Hindu teachers heard.
Smrithi	The materials of *Sruti* explained among the pioneers of Hindu teachers
Vedas	The Primary/ Authentic Hindu Scriptures. There are four Vedas and its interpretations, together called Vedas.
Rig Veda	The first *veda* of Hindus
Yajur Veda	The second *veda* of Hindus
Sama Veda	The third *veda* of Hindus
Atharva	The fourth *veda* of Hindus
Adivasis	The original or ancient people of the land.
Hindu Dharma	Ethos/ Ethics of Hinduism
Panchamas	Fifth Caste
Karma Theory	Hindus considers the Actions of the previous life effects a person through out the present life.
Bahujan Samaj	People's society
punarjanma	rebirth
samsara	Transmigration of the soul
punya	merit
moksha	Salvation
Thirukulattar,	People of Holy Clan

Glossary

Adi	first, original
Avatar	incarnation
Balutedar	village public servant
Barkat	material blessing
Begar	forced labour
Bhakti	devotion to God
Cheri	separate hamlet inhabited by Dalits on the edge of the village
Dacoit	robber, bandi
Dasas	literally 'slaves'; Aryan word for the inhabitation of India they conquered
Devata	goddess
Dharma	sacred moral and religious duties prescribed for each caste
Dharmsala	places of worship. Also places where pilgrims can spend the night
Faqir	Muslim ascetic
Ghat	place for bathing
Gotra	clan or lineage group within a caste
Gur	molasses
Guru	spiritual preceptor
Harijan Seva Sangh	Society of those serving Dalits
Jajmani	hereditary patron-servant relationship of a dominant caste family with a lower caste family
Jati	an endogamous caste unity

Karma	a person's fate or destiny as determined by his/her actions in a previous life
Khudawand Yisu	Lord Jesus
Kisan Sabha	peasant organization
Lakh	100,000
Lambardar	village headman
Lok Sabha	Lower House of the Indian Parliament similar to the British House of Commons
Mantra	religious incantation
Mazhabi Sikhs	Those Chuhras who are Sikh by religion
Mela	fair
Panchama	those belonging to the 'fifth' varna, a term for Dalits
Panchayat	a council of five members
Puja	worship, often with offerings to the deity
Rajayoga	practitioner of yoga according to Pitanjali's Yoga Shastra
Rajya Sabha	Upper House of the Indian Parliament
Ryotwari	land revenue settlement between the stae and the peasant cultivator
Sabha	assembly or society
Sahitya	literature
Samaj	society
Sanatani	upholders of the eternal moral and religious duties
Sangam	literary academy of ancient South India

Satyagraha	literally truth force, Gandhi's method of non-violent protest
Shuddhi	purification, a rite used by the Arya Samaj
Varna	literally colour, broad categories into which jatis were classified
Varnashrama Dharma	The social order based on varnas carrying out their respective Dharma
Community	A corporate body sharing sociological identity and a geographic area.
Culture	It is the sum total of integrated, Institutionalised, non-instinctive and learned behaviour patterns of people over space and time.
Ethnolinguistic-	People Identified ethnic group speaking the same language.
Evangelism	The activity of sharing the good news of Jesus Christ with someone clearly enough for them to understand and accept Him.
Evangelization	Reaching en entire group or city or country with the gospel.
Homogenous	People of having similar characteristics in a community or society.
Indigenous	aboriginal or native, pertaining to the original Inhabitants of a region.
Lineage	It is unilateral kinship group that traces, Descent from known common ancestor and is always exogamous.
Religion	The shared beliefs and belief practices of a People group.

Introduction

Indian society is arranged according to the caste system—a unique Indian phenomenon, a religious system sanctioned and sustained by Hinduism. For the sociologist Louis Dumont, the caste system is inconceivable apart from the Hindu context. The caste system is not a form of social stratification but a social problem, or the mother of all evils of Indian society. "It is the most baneful, hard hearted and cruel social system that could possibly be invented for damaging the human race." The philosophy or the religious doctrine of Hinduism is not based on the principle of justice; it is against the principle of liberty, equality and fraternity. The caste system is a form of apartheid.

The Christian Church in India, in a predominantly Hindu environment, has succumbed to the process of uncritical enculturation and is practicing caste in the lives of churches as well as Christians. Today, we are becoming aware of the unchristian side of the Christian church. For some, the practice of caste in the Church amounts to apostasy from the Christian faith. So there is an urgency to recover our tradition of faith and to permit that tradition to permeate our Christian vocation. The Scriptures continue to march through contemporary history, shaking and shaping it, so that God's justice may give His people, the Dalits, the righteousness they so direly need.

The faith we exercise in God convincingly and continually reminds us that the Creator God created people equally and in His own image. The same God continues to love all His created people equally. This gives us the basic responsibility to defend the rights of any people group that is suppressed and denied any of their human rights and dignity.[1] Theology is a political language. What people think about God, Jesus Christ and the Church cannot be separated from their own social and political status in a given society. Dalit Theology is an attempt towards an authentically Indian liberation theology. The emerging and experimental nature of Dalit Theology seems to suggest a degree of innovation and a willingness on the part of theologians to explore new ideas. It suggests that while still developing, some of the judgments and hypotheses of Dalit[2] Theology are to be tested in the light of historical research.

Corresponding to liberation theologies, Dalit Theology is based on social analysis and empirical investigation. Dalit Liberation Theology begins with the present historical reality rather than with Scripture or Christian tradition. Consequently, Dalit Theology is considered to be a counter theological movement. Liberation theologians maintain discontinuity with the dominant theological traditions of Europe and North America. Dalit theologians insist on a radical discontinuity with traditional Indian Christian Theology.

Dalit Theology is an emerging theology and it is in the process of development in the realms of politics, economics, social structure and culture, as it has gained a powerful entry into sociological and theological writings. It is rightly remarked that "being an indigenous theology, it is more contextual and "human-hood" "praxis oriented."[3] Similar to liberation theologians, Dalit theologians claim methodological exclusivism for Dalit Theology and assert that the articulation of Dalit Theology is a new way of doing theology. They contend that it a theology from below. It begins with the

---

[1] James H. Cone, "The Social Context of Theology" in Choan Sengsong (ed.), *Doing Theology Today* (Madras: CLIS, 1976), 38.

[2] *Ibid.*, p.39

[3] T. Aruldoss, *Why Dalit Theology?* (Madurai: J & D Publications, 1997), p. 1.

poor and the oppressed. Like the Black and other liberation theologies, Dalit Liberation Theology arises from the pains of poverty and oppression. These theologies recognise God's presence in the struggle to get rid of oppression. The experience of the poor and the oppressed, such as Black and Dalits, is the hermeneutical starting point. The term "caste" is still in practice in government, public sector and society. In government records for people identification, there is a caste column to be filled by the people either in schools or in the job requirement department. In some states in our country, the caste name is used as surname for people. Although the caste system in India is banned by the government in record, it is widely in practice. So the writer is compelled to use the term "caste" in this book.

Statement of Purpose

Indian society is arranged according to the caste system. Among the Hindus, the stratification of caste division is used to justify inequalities. The dominant caste is the promoter of this evil in order to control and manipulate other castes for their motives. The system forcibly divides work and entrusts all risky jobs to the lower castes without giving proper wages. Moreover, they are not permitting the new generations of the lower castes to train themselves to uplift their social status. It was so much before the arrival of Western Colonial powers. However, after the arrival of Western colonial power and Western Christian missions, we could see promotion of lower castes at least among the centres of Christian missions. Even then, we could see the continuity and rigidity of this social evil among the Hindu and Christian communities.

Although the caste system is a Hindu system, we see its effect and influence among the Christians who live among the Hindus. According to the sociologist Louis Dumont, the caste system is inconceivable apart from the Hindu context. The caste system is not a form of social stratification but a social problem, or the mother of all evils of Indian society.[4] Sherings says, "It is the most baneful, hard hearted and cruel social system that could possibly be invented for damaging the human race."[5] The philosophy or the religious doctrine of Hinduism is not based on the principle of justice; it is against the principle of liberty, equality and fraternity. The caste system is a form of apartheid.

The Christian church in India, in a predominantly Hindu environment, has succumbed to the process of uncritical enculturation and is practicing caste in the lives of churches as well as Christians. Today, we are becoming aware of the unchristian side of the Christian church. For some, the practice of caste in the church amounts to apostasy from the Christian faith. So there is an urgency to recover our Christian tradition of faith and to permit that tradition to permeate our Christian vocation. Dalit Christians are two times untouchables — before conversion, in the Hindu society, and after conversion, in the Christian society. This is the time to deliver Dalit Christians from the physical and spiritual bondage through the Gospel of Jesus Christ. The writer believes any attempts at Dalit Theology will have to pay attention to the Dalit reality as a whole — with its historical, cultural, social, economic, political, theological and artistic aspects.

In this study, the writer tries to recover the biblical vision in order that this might orient us towards an authentic Christian discipleship and thereby challenge us to work towards the dismantling of the caste system that undergirds and makes possible an oppressive culture.

Goals of the Research

This book is an attempt at moving towards the construction of Dalit Theology exclusively for the liberation of the Dalit

---

[4] Keer, *Dr. Ambedkar Life and Mission*, p. 3.

[5] A. Ramaiah, "The Dalit Issue: A Hindu Perspective," in Jams Massey (ed.) *Indigenous People: Dalits – Dalit Issues in Today's Theological Debate* (Delhi: ISPCK, 1994), pp. 79-80.

people in India. It focuses on the physical and spiritual freedom that Dalit Christians should have—freedom that can be attained through Jesus Christ, who says in John's Gospel, "Then you will know the truth, and the truth will set you free." So, if the Son sets you free, you will be free indeed. Ultimately, the study tries to lead the Christians into transforming themselves according to biblical values. Thus, they would be motivated to transform society.

Significance of the Research

The Christian Church in India lives in a predominantly Hindu environment. The educated Hindus in India consider the caste system as a social evil. The lower-caste people in India agitate with all their strength to come out of the social evil of the caste system. They consider the caste system as a form of apartheid. We can see the heredity of Indian Christianity from the first century of its birth. However, Christians could not influence the major Hindu society in India. One of the major reasons is negligence of Christians to participate in social transformation through the life and witness of the Church. Although many lower-caste Hindus were attracted to Christian missions during the era of western missions, they were not satisfactorily accepted among the national Christian communities in India. Now the time has gone for the Christian Church to change the method and approach of mission and contextualisation.

The Christian Church has succumbed to the process of uncritical enculturation and is practicing caste in the lives of churches as well as Christians. Today, we are becoming aware of the un-Christian side of the Christian Church. For some, the practice of caste in the Church amounts to apostasy from the Christian faith. So there is an urgency to recover our Christian tradition of faith and to permit that tradition to permeate our Christian vocation.

Scope and Methodology

The scope of the proposed study is limited to the majority of the poor and oppressed who make up the Dalits in India. The Christian Church has failed to take account of the sufferings and hope of the Dalits. The Christian approach as a response to the philosophical, theological conceptions of the dominant Brahmanical religion and culture has not helped Dalit aspirations. The researcher in this study tries to recover through the biblical vision the battered identity and Christian history of the Dalits by awakening the Church to an awareness of the poor and oppressed and their subsequent transformation. The Christian Church should change its method and approach of mission and contextualization. The book will focus on this issue. We will also analyse terms such as "Dalits", "Dalit Theology", "Inculturalisation" and "Syncretism", as these terms will have a bearing on the contextualisation of Dalit Theology. However, a detailed treatment of these terms is beyond the scope of this study.

The main theme of the research is that though the Christian mission did contribute to the awakening of the depressed classes and the consciousness of these people, which resulted in their socio-economic transformation, the Church today is practicing caste within its structures. This study tries to orient us in the light of the biblical vision towards authentic Christian discipleship and thereby challenge us to work towards the dismantling of the caste system that undergirds and makes possible an oppressive culture in Indian Church and society.

The researcher has made a study of the caste system in India, its roots and how the Dalits were considered as the oppressed people. The study traces similar theologies and develops Dalit Theology, articulating a genuine contextual theology rooted in Dalit Christian history.

Hypothesis and Limitations

The research problem is being proposed for a number of reasons. Firstly, Dalit Theology relates to the experiences and expressions of the people who are excluded in society; it refers to their struggles for social justice and their search for a meaningful life in community. The missionary endeavour did contribute to the awakening of the Dalit consciousness and personal dignity. There was a social change and upward social mobility. Though there has been a transformation among these neglected people of society, today the Church treats them just the same as before. The research examines the Christian mission contribution to Dalit consciousness and identity and evaluates the liberation of the Dalits in the present-day context.

The present study, by giving due consideration to the Christian mission contribution to Dalit consciousness and identity, has the potential to contribute to a fuller understanding of transforming the Dalits in Indian society. Secondly, the investigation of the various related theologies brings into focus the larger question of the relationship of the Church to the history of the neglected and oppressed people. Thirdly, the present study brings out the correlation between biblical values and the socio-culturally discriminated lower strata of people. It is hoped that this study will enlighten us about the caste system and give us some insights into the contextualisation of Dalit Theology in contemporary Indian society, which is marked by many millions of poor and oppressed people. The Dalit theologians advocate total transformation of the whole Dalit society, whereas the missionaries preferred planting Christian congregations, building communities and erecting big churches. This investigation examines the question thus raised of how to bring change in society, especially among the poor and the disadvantaged.

This research is limited in scope to the Dalits. The researcher has relied for most part of the thesis on library resources. Primary sources were not readily available at times. Wherever such sources were not available, the study relied on secondary sources. Since we are aiming at constructing Dalit Theology and developing it in the Indian Church and Society, the study uses textual sources to meet that end. Secondly, the research deals with the Dalit methodology of experience and consciousness. Therefore, the descriptions of them are a sincere attempt to articulate and visualise as people understand it. The researcher has used methodological tools such as history of casteism, description of the Dalits, experience of the sufferings of the Dalits and consciousness of transforming the Dalits to articulate the phenomena that would describe the oppression of the Dalits. Nevertheless, the investigation of the research will illumine us about the transformation of the lives of the Dalits.

Definitions of Terms

Dalits

The word "Dalit" means oppressed; at present, it refers only to the exuntouchables of India who are known as depressed classes or Harijans (children of God) and Scheduled Castes (SCs). So, M. E. Prabhakar writes, "Dalits", in a wider sense, would include all the oppressed people; However, in current parlance, such Dalits would refer exclusively to the ethnic communities making up almost one-fifth of the total population, popularly called "Harijans" (children of God) and placed outside the caste system because of their being considered outcaste and untouchable, who are by legislation listed under Scheduled Castes (needing protective discrimination by the state).

Dalits are the "enduring groups" of castes, the people who have endured oppression more than any other. Dalits are oppressed because they are "born", or "branded" with the stigma of untouchability. The word "Dalit" has been used to identify those communities that have been economically, socially and politically oppressed for centuries by the Brahminical Hindu social order, that is, the caste system.

The term "caste" is still in practice in government, public sector and society. In government records for people identification, there is a caste column to be filled by the people either at schools or in the job requirement department. In some states in our country, the caste name is used as surname for the people. Although the caste system in India has been banned by the government in record, it is still in practice. So, the writer is compelled to use the term 'caste' in this book.

Dalit Theology

The emerging and experimental nature of Dalit Theology seems to suggest a degree of innovation and a willingness on the part of theologians to explore new ideas. It suggests that while still developing, some of the judgments and hypotheses of Dalit Theology are to be tested in the light of historical research.

Dalit Theology is a new way of doing theology. They contend that it a theology from below. It begins with the poor and the oppressed. Like the Black and other liberation theologies, Dalit liberation theology arises from the pains of poverty and oppression. These theologies recognise God's presence in the struggle to get rid of oppression. The experience of the poor and the oppressed, such as the Black and the Dalits, is the hermeneutical starting point.

Dalit Theology is based on social analysis and empirical investigation. Dalit Theology runs counter to the existing Indian Christian theology, which has been articulated mostly by upper-caste theologians who they claim ignored the interests of the Dalits.

Inculturalisation

Inculturalisation is the incarnation of Christian life and of the Christian message in a particular cultural context, in such a way that this experience not only finds expression through elements proper to the culture in question, but also becomes a principle that animates, directs and unifies the culture, transforming and remaking it so as to bring about "a new creation."

Luzbetak remarks that inculturalisation refers to translating the concepts of the gospel in a new cultural setting by outsiders; it refers to the insiders of the culture integrating at the root of their culture, values, ideals, teachings and orientation of the gospel and Church tradition.

Syncretism

This means blending of one idea, practice or attitude with another. Traditionally, among Christians, it has been used for the replacement or dilution of the essential truths of the gospel through the incorporation of non-Christian elements. Syncretism of some form has been seen everywhere the Church existed. In syncretism, alternative religious practices or the understanding that is replaced by the essential elements of the gospel is exposed and challenged.

Dalit Consciousness

It was a constant reminder of their age-old oppression and their ancient glorious past, when their forefathers were a free people. This has become an expression of hope for them in recovering and enhancing their past identity by expressing their sufferings through drama and poetry. The Maharastra movement, which has been producing Dalit literature since the 1970s, has been said to be a protest in nature as its main theme is total human liberation. Its hero was B. R. Ambedkar.

Contextualisation

The term "contextualisation" is used in this series to denote "the efforts of formulating, presenting and practicing the Christian faith in such a way that is relevant to the cultural context of the target group in terms of conceptualization, expression and application; yet maintaining theological coherence, biblical integrity and theoretical consistency."[6]

Outline of the Study

The proposed study will be based on the resources that are directly or indirectly related to the Dalits. The first chapter analyses casteism in India; it traces the origin and development of the caste system in Ancient India and proceeds to Modern Indian Reform Movements, which tried to annihilate the caste system in India. The second chapter deals with the Dalits who were regarded as fifth-grade people in the hierarchy of the caste system in India. This chapter traces the origin of the Dalits, their sufferings as an oppressed community. It also deals with leaders like Mahatma Gandhi, B. R. Ambedkar and E. V. Ramaswamy Naicker, who fought for the Dalit cause. The third chapter deals with similar types of theologies, which throw light on the liberation of the suffering people. The fourth chapter examines towards constructing Dalit Theology for Dalit liberation and the different sources that were used in making Dalit Theology. The fifth chapter deals with the implication of Dalit Theology for the liberation of Dalit people in India. This is followed by conclusions and a brief discussion about the relevance of the study for the Indian context.

---

[6] Wan, "Critiquing the Method of Traditional Western Theology and Calling for Sino-Theology."

Chapter 1

Caste System in India

About 3,500 years ago, a group from Central Asia entered India in search of a land to occupy and to make a living. Those Aryans who came to India established their dominance over the indigenous people who had been living here. They created thousands of gods and goddesses, their horoscope, the Vedas and the Upanishads and claimed that these were their sacred Scriptures. Caste is an offspring of racism. It has emanated from a racist ideology. Caste is a social division of an unequal order within one race. In its essence, as a dogma, it excludes the Dalit people from the caste division of society, as they are from a different race.

Background of the Caste System

The caste system has a dogmatic virtue around the denial of education to the Dalits. It is prohibited in the holy books of Hinduism. Lack of economic sustainability of the family is a major cause of the denial of educational rights. Lack of security for Dalit girls to reach school and reach back home denies their right to education. Open discrimination of Dalit students by students and teachers at schools and colleges and the denial of a learning environment lead to a greater denial of educational rights. Privatisation of education has led to further denial of educational opportunities to the Dalits. Caste discrimination is widespread in India even today, though the Constitution of India has banned it.

Caste Division

In India, 64 per cent are caste Hindus, 14 per cent are Harijan (Dalits), 7 per cent are tribals, 12 per cent are Muslims and just 3 per cent are Christians. Caste division is a system that pervasively influences every religion in India to a lesser or greater extent. It is fundamental to Hinduism. Caste discrimination is forbidden by the Constitution, but it is socially important for over 80 per cent of the population. Dhananjay Keer rightly observes, "The Vedic Aryans knew no caste system. As time went on, the Aryans divided themselves for different occupations on the basis of divisions of labour and according to aptitude, liking and capacity of the individual."[1]

Origin and Development

In tracing the origins of caste, people are handicapped by the lack of written records. The Aryans, a series of related and highly self-conscious tribes sharing a common language and religion, began their invasions of India from the northwest around 1500 B.C. For centuries, they remained in seemingly constant conflict with the indigenous peoples, whom the Aryans looked down upon as culturally inferior and excluded as ritually unclean.

The origin of the caste system, called Varnashrama, was legitimate and virtuous. It was meant for the progressive organisation of society. Varnashrama is the Vedic system that divides society into four natural groups, depending on individual characteristics and dispositions. Everyone has certain tendencies by their own natural inclinations and choice. These inclinations are also seen in one's occupational preferences. These activities are divided into four basic divisions called *varnas*. For example, there are those who prefer to offer service to society through physical labour or working for others, i.e., shudras; those who serve through agriculture, trade, commerce, business and banking or administrative work, i.e., Vaishyas; those who have the talents of leaders, government administration, police or military and the protection of society, i.e., Kshatriyas; and those who are by nature intellectuals, contemplative and

---

[1] Dhananjay Keer, *Dr. Ambedkar Life and Mission* (Bombay: Popular Prakashan, 1994), p. 2.

inspired by acquiring spiritual and philosophical knowledge and motivated to work in this way for the rest of society, i.e., Brahmanas. "It was never a factor of whether a person had a certain ancestry or birth that determined which class was most appropriate for him or her."[2] Through time, society began to divide according to the caste system.

Brahmins—Cause of the Caste System

The Brahmins as a caste are responsible for establishing the caste system in India as a social order that governs the systems of the country. One of the major projects of Brahminisation is the establishment of the caste system as a social order in India. S. Radhakrishnan, who is acknowledged as one of the best Indian philosophers, observes the origin of the caste system thus:

> The Purusa Sukta has the first reference to the division of Hindu society into the four classes. To understand the natural ways, in which this institution arose, we must remember that the Aryan conquerors were divided by differences of blood and racial ancestry from the conquered tribes of India. The original Aryans all belonged to one class, every one being priest and soldier, trader and tiller of the soil. The complexity of life led to a division of classes among the Aryans.[3]

According to Babasaheb Ambedkar, there is no difference of castes; this world, having been at first created by Brahma, entirely Brahmanic, became separated into castes in consequence of works.

> Those Brahmans who were fond of sensual pleasure, fiery, irascible, prone to violence, had forsaken their duty and were red-limbed, fell into the condition of Kshatriyas. Those Brahmans who derived their livelihood from kine, who were yellow, who subsisted by agriculture, and who neglected to practice their duties, entered into state of Vaishyas. Those Brahmans, who were addicted to mischief and falsehood, who were covetous, who lived by all kinds of works, who were black and had fallen from purity, sank into the condition of Sudras. Being separated from each other by these works, the Brahmans became divided into different castes.[4]

---

[2] Stephen Knapp, "Casteism: Is It the Scourge of Hinduism, or the Perversion of a Legitimate Vedic System?" http://www.stephen-knapp.com

[3] S. Radhakrishnan, *Indian Philosophy*, vol. 1, Pp. 111-112.

[4] Babasaheb Ambedkar, *Writings and Speeches*, Vol. 5, Pp. 193-194.

The Indo-Aryan society has an official gradation laid down; fixed and permanent with an ascending scale of reverence and a descending scale of contempt. "The scheme of the Purusha Sukta is unique in as much as it has fixed a permanent warrant of precedence neither time nor circumstances can alter."[5]

The Aryans came here, applied the policy of "divide and rule", "propounded the theory of casteism and converted all those ten tribes into about 6,000 castes and also sowed the seeds of discrimination among the native people."[6]

The Brahminic order has been trying with Dalit identity as it liked. Originally, when the caste system came into being in India, the Dalit people were clubbed into the Shudra identity. Shudra then was an identity for all those who did not belong to the three castes that were identified within the gambit of the caste system.

Characteristics of the Caste System

Indian society is primarily a caste-based society. The caste system continues to be a fact of life in India that dominates interpersonal and inter-group relations. The categories of caste and class, though closely related, are distinct and in a way, worlds apart. Caste is based on birth; it offers ascribed status. It is group-based, rigid and fixed. It is based on religious foundations and determined by the *karma* theory. The principle that manifests in caste society is the principle of complementarities. "The evil system of casteism has degraded, segregated and devitalized the Hindu society."[7] One of the earlier reports observes aptly, "The real triumph of the caste system lies not on upholding the supremacy of the Brahmin, but in conditioning the consciousness of the

---

[5] T H P Chentharassery, *Ambedkar on Indian History*, p. 41.

[6] Subhas Chandra Musafir, "A Section of Educated Dalits have Become Mini-Brahmins", *Dalit Voice*, July 15-31, 1999, p. 22.

[7] Keer, *Dr. Ambedkar Life and Mission*, p. 3.

Lower Castes in accepting their inferior status in the ritual hierarchy as part of the natural order of things."[8]

Features of the Caste System

Caste distinctions are part of Indian society, and by no means, are they peculiar to India. He recognises in the principles of caste an authority similar to that which the Ten Commandments have for Christians. He would be commended as progressive if he was to break caste, but he might feel that he had acted contrary to the nature of things. Even a staunch Hindu and a great philosopher-statesman like Dr. S. Radhakrishnan has said that caste is the source of division and misfortune.[9]

Casteism in India received a lot of criticism, and rightly so. Casteism, as we find it today, is now nothing more than a misrepresentation and misinterpretation of a legitimate and progressive Vedic system known as *varnashrama*. However, we need to know the difference between the two and then get rid of present-day casteism to again utilise the genuine and liberal form of social organisation, known as *varnashrama*.[10]

At the end of the Vedic period, the Varna system began to modify itself into the "caste system" that divides the entire Indian population into various endogamous groups with varying social status.

> Those who are born in one group can never become member of any other group. They assume the social status or social identity of the group in which they are born and thereafter they hardly have any scope to alter their given identity.[11]

---

[8] Report of the Backward Classes Commission, Government of India, First Part, Vol. I & II, 1980, p.14.

[9] Report in the *Bulletin of the Institute of Traditional Cultures*, Madras University, 1980.

[10] Stephen Knapp, "Casteism" in http://www.stephen-knapp.com

[11] A. Ramaiah, "The Dalit Issue: A Hindu Perspective," in James Massey (ed.) *Indigenous People: Dalits – Dalit Issues in Today's Theological Debate* (Delhi: ISPCK, 1994), pp. 79-80.

Despite the fact that there will not be much evidence of the caste in the casual contacts, many Indians are aware of the injustice that is implied in a rigid application of caste. The government has officially outlawed untouchability and has given to the outcastes the new name of Harijan, which means 'children of god.' Henceforth, caste is to be no barrier to promotion, and no provision is to be made for separate dining in pubic eating-places. Such regulations mitigate the hardships imposed by caste. "The early Baptist missionaries at Serampore saw caste as a prison far stronger than any which the civil tyrannies of the world have erected, a prison which immunes many innocent beings."[12]

In casteism, birth is now a major factor in determining one's social standing. It dictates that your social order, occupational potential and characteristics are the same as your parents, which is a label that may have been placed on a family hundreds of years ago.[13]

What Manckiam points out is very much applicable to most of the rural areas:

> Caste has killed public spirit; caste has destroyed the sense of public charity. Caste has made public opinion impossible. A Hindu's public life is caste. His responsibility is only to his caste. His loyalty is restricted only to his caste. Virtue has become caste-ridden and morality has become caste-bound.[14]

Massey points out that "the caste is primarily religious, a stumbling block in the spread of the gospel, different from social rank, and hampers morality and advancement."[15]

"Upper castes Hindus have a vested interest in maintaining and perpetuating caste. If caste goes, Hinduism

---

[12] Daniel Potts, *British Baptist Missionaries in India* (Cambridge: Friend Of India, 1967), p. 158.

[13] Stephen Knapp, "Casteism" in http://www.stephen-knapp.com

[14] *Ibid.*, p. 60.

[15] Godwin Shiri, "Glimpses from the 19th century – Missionary Crusade Against Caste: Lessons for Doing Theology Today", in Samson Prabahakar and Jinkwan Kwon (eds.) *Dalit and Minjung Theologies - A Dialogue* (Bangalore: BTESSC/SATHRI, 2006), pp. 25-27.

will die. With the Dalits, it is just the opposite. Caste is the greatest obstacle in the way of their unity and progress."[16]

Caste and Untouchability

Untouchability and caste are mental constructs of a diabolic mind, specifically aimed at taking away all the resources of the country and subjugating the people in return. Brahminism produced innumerable discourses for the establishment of untouchability as a divine order for the peaceful running of society. Dalits do not believe in untouchability. The core value of Dalitism is inclusiveness. Therefore, untouchability is outside the purview of a Dalit worldview. In its very construction, untouchability is negative. To identify a people as untouchables is the worst things than can happen to human civilisation.

Bhagwan Das gives the main cause of practicing untouchability as he says, "Untouchability has been practiced in the Hindu society for centuries. Various reasons are given justifying the practice. Main causes were the obsession of the Brahmins to maintain purity and to avoid pollution."[17]

Untouchability is metaphysical. Untouchability is suffered both in the mind and in the body. The effect of the discourse of purity-impurity and pollution falls on the Dalit community as a whole. The cause of untouchability is the Brahmin mindset. It welcomes the untouchability of a particular community of Dalits.

The identity of the Dalits is not one of being poor. It is one of being oppressed in the name of an ascribed caste identity. Untouchability is the worst type of oppression that the Dalit people have experienced, as it has denied them their humanity and has been worse than slavery.

---

[16] Bhagwan Das, "Dalits and the Caste System," in James Massey (ed.) *Indigenous People: Dalits – Dalit Issues in Today's Theological Debate* (Delhi: ISPCK, 1994), p. 61.

[17] *Ibid.,* p. 75.

Structure

The caste system is a uniquely Indian system of social stratification found only in India and the neighbouring countries, such as Sri Lanka, Nepal, Pakistan and Bangladesh, to which Hindus have migrated. It is a comprehensive system incorporating socio-economic and political as well as religio-cultural dimensions of Indian context.

Brahmins

The Brahmin comes from the head of Brahma. The head is ascribed a superiority because of its thinking function. By implication it means that feeling is an inferior function. Those who have knowledge have the highest status in society and religion. By implication, it means that those who have been denied the opportunity to acquire knowledge will be treated low in society. Brahmins, having emanated from the head of Brahma, have the karma of learning, acquiring knowledge and teaching. The profession of the Brahmin is to acquire knowledge and do all such things that are related to the realm of knowledge.

Kshatriyas

The next caste people who are a grade lower emanate from the shoulders of Brahma. They are the Kshatriyas, the warriors. Even today, in modern battle, shoulders are crucial. For bow and arrow, shoulders are essential. The Kshatriyas have the karma of fighting in the battlefield. The consequence of one's action is not the responsibility of the subject who acts but belongs to the karma of the object. The Kshatriya's profession is to fight in the battlefield.

Vaishyas

The next ones in the caste ladder are the Vaishyas. These are the traders. In those days, as it is these days in many parts of the world, the traders had to move form place to place to mobilise raw materials as well as to sell their products. Thighs were the focal point for the trader's movement to different places. Since the Vaishyas have originated from the thighs of Brahma, their karma is to trade and make a living. It is their profession.

Shudras

Shudras is the next caste found in the caste ladder. They originate from the feet of Brahma. The feet, though used primarily for seasoning the land for cultivation, are also used for multiple purposes. Those who made cultivation as their profession, the farmers, are primarily Shudras. Those who played a supportive role to the farmers, such as the carpenter and the blacksmith, were also Shudras. Not only they, but also all those who did all sorts of menial jobs belong to this last grade in the caste.

Castes in Modern India

Indian society is not only a multi-racial, multi-religious and multi-lingual society, but also a caste-ridden society. It divides the people as superior and inferior, pure and impure. This division begins from one's birth and goes up to the funeral pyre. "It stands as a symbol of evil especially in the lives of the Dalits because it considers the Dalits as outcastes and no people and segregates them from the rest."[18]

Castes and Ideology

In India, there are almost as many ways of life as there are castes. Casteism says that if you are born into a Brahmana family, then you are a Brahmana, no matter whether you truly exhibit the genuine characteristics of a brahmana or not. If you are born into a Kshatriya family or a Vaishya or Shudra family, then that is what you must be.

The Dalitness in the Dalits will necessarily lead to the removal of their Dalit identity as an oppressed people in the name of caste. They cannot be called untouchable, if untouchability is removed. They cannot be called an oppressed people if there is no more oppression. However,

---

[18] Aruldoss, *Why Dalit Theology?*, p. 5.

Dalitism, as a philosophy of liberation from oppression and exploitation of the dominant caste forces will continue to guide the destiny of societies in liberty, equality and fraternity.

For Kanshi Ram, "there were only two categories of the Indians – the first one were the beneficiaries of the vicious social system and the others were the victims of this system."[19] Like his mentor, Dr. B.R. Ambedkar, he was aware that political power is the key to all social progress.

> He was convinced that apart from politics, Dalit empowerment was not possible. The Scheduled Castes, the Scheduled Tribes, The Backward Castes, the Muslims, Buddhists, Sikh, were Christians were brought together under one banner.[20]

The lower castes do not have written codes but have framed rules, reserved by the older people and passed on to the next generation orally or through tradition so as to regulate their caste relations. Relations are determined on the basis of the treatment meted out by the upper caste people.[21]

The very touch of a Dalit is considered as pollution and defilement, and even the proximity or falling of his shadow is considered impure. Being an offshoot of the caste system, the stigma of untouchability is also extended to various fields. As a result, the Dalits are debarred from using public roads, particularly in the rural areas, although the roads are maintained by the government for which the Dalits are also contributing by way of various taxes. When the Dalits attempted to use these roads and wanted to assert their rights, 'they faced the utmost ignominy and humiliation by the upper caste people.[22]

What Srikhant points out in his report is worth noting here:

---

[19] Ambrose Pinto, "Kanshi Ram: A Challenge to NGOs" *Indian Currents,* 30 Oct,-Nov. 2006, pp. 19-20.

[20] *Ibid.,* p. 20.

[21] Das, "Dalits and the Caste System," p. 66.

[22] Aruldoss, *Why Dalit Theology?* , p. 6.

> Caste in Hindu society is still the most powerful factor in determining a man's dignity, calling or profession. Such a rigid caste-system is not found anywhere else outside India, all such professions involve handling of him so-called dirty jobs like tanning and skinning of hides, manufacture of leather goods, sweeping of streets, scavenging, etc. are allocated to some castes also known as Harijan...[23]

It is an ideology that believes in treating people contemptuously. It is an ideology that denies human dignity to people as a religious dogma. Prabhakar rightly observes that:

> The principles and practices of caste are rooted in the religious-philosophical-theological traditions of the dominant Hindu culture. The system of Varna, ritual ranking, provides the doctrinal basis for hierarchy and discrimination between jatis or castes and exclusion of certain 'impure' castes as untouchables and outcastes.[24]

The caste system deprives people of ambition towards progress and change; it leaves one to be content with one's position in life and against elevation to high position to which one is fitted. Personal status for life is determined by the rank of the group to which one belongs. "We are bound to say then that inequality is also the result of the caste system, which is in turn the principal product of Hindu civilization."[25]

The doctrine of karma, which taught that the good and evil deeds of a person automatically influence his state in future lives, the concomitant doctrines of *punarjanma* (rebirth) and the endless cycle of *samsara* (transmigration of the soul) to build up *punya* (merit) by works, to obtain *moksha* or final deliverance (salvation) are further added to it.[26]

---

[23] Shrikant, L. M. "Report of the Commissioner for Scheduled Castes and Scheduled Tribes for the period ending 31st December 1951," p. 1.

[24] M. E. Prabhakar, "The Search for a Dalit Theology," in James Massey (ed.), *Indigenous People: Dalits – Dalit Issues in Today's Theological Debate* (Delhi: ISPCK, 1994), p. 203.

[25] Manickam, Studies in Missionary History, p. 59.

[26] M. E. Prabahkar, "Christology in Dalit Perspective," in V. Devasahayam (ed.), *Frontiers of Dalit Theology* (Delhi: ISPCK, 1997), p. 406.

Caste discrimination and untouchability cannot be removed by good intentions or even by legislation, until they are disapproved and disallowed under religious sanctions, considering that caste and caste ideology are based on religious dogma.

Attitude towards Caste

As casteism continues, it furthers the fragmentation of Indian society. In fact, it has brought about the numerous divisions and social quarrels that we now find in India. Even amongst the Hindus alone, there has been fighting along caste, ethnic and sectarian lines for hundreds of years. This is one of the main reasons why the country has been weakened to such a degree that they could not properly defend themselves in a unified way from the genocide under the Muslim invasions and modern fundamentalism. This sort of fragmentation also forced Indians to endure two centuries of British persecutions.[27]

Casteism today does not help society advance spiritually. In fact, it helps promote contempt and disapproval among the people of different classes and ethnic groups. For this reason, we still see today that when the Shudras and the Dalits feel like they are disliked by fellow Hindus, they become Muslims or Christians or Buddhists in an attempt to find greater acceptance and avoid class distinctions. The result of this has been social disharmony. Otherwise, there would have been no need for parts of India to be divided to create Bangladesh and Pakistan, which — especially Pakistan — have since become nothing more than mortal enemies of India. Ethnic intolerance is on the rise in many parts of India.[28]

Even today, you can find such divisions that a brahmana from one state does not trust a brahmana from a different part of India. For example, the Nambudris of Kerala look down on other brahmanas. Even among other groups, a Jat

---

[27] Knapp, "Casteism in   http://www.stephen-knapp.com

[28] *Ibid.*

boy from the Punjab will not marry a Jat girl from Uttar Pradesh. A Patel from Kutch will regard a Patel from Ahmedabad as a foreigner. Thus, the problem of caste and ethnicity is making a society that fights like cats and dogs. In reality, casteism is killing Indian culture.[29]

Everywhere Dalits continue to suffer because of various forms of discrimination. What the Dalits look for is a real and total resurrection that will finally liberate them from the clutches of caste discrimination, and certainly not just a bandage for their wounds. The Dalits are demanding their rights and human dignity and the high caste people are insisting upon their hegemony.

Castes and Power

The forces of globalization, especially the economic bodies, have usurped the powers of allocation by blurring the political borders of the nation-state. The cultural nationalism of the caste leaders of India has sought to establish power as dominance. According to it, the business of governance belongs to a certain caste group. The determining factor is birth in a particular dominant caste. By proposing a three-pronged strategy of educating, agitating and organising, Ambedkar advocated power as resistance. One of the things that Hinduism has bequeathed to the Christian Church in India is the institution of caste, which is in essence an integral part of Hinduism. When coverts first came from paganism and Hindu background into the pale of Christianity, some of the early missionaries, being anxious to win converts, particularly from high caste Hindus, admitted them without asking to renounce caste, "the badge of idolatry."[30]

Caste in Power

According to it, the business of governance belongs to a certain caste group. The determining factor is birth in a

---

[29] *Ibid.*

[30] William Campbell, *British India in its Relations to the Decline of Hindooism and the progress of Christianity* (London: n.p., 1839), p. 162.

particular dominant caste. By proposing a three-pronged strategy of educating, agitating and organising, Ambedkar advocated power as resistance.[31]

Political powers still have not had a heavy focus on what should be happening outside of a community, in the larger context, to capture political power. India is not one nation as one can see in many other nations. India is a continent of nations. Each state of India has a different language and a different culture. Indigenous people groups, such as the tribals, do not belong to the Hindu religion.

Bharat Putra aptly observes:

> The fact that casteism has been in existence for hundreds of years does not square with the court's observation that 'reservation is necessary for transcending caste and not for perpetuating it. Reservation has to be used in a limited sense; otherwise it will perpetuate casteism in the country.'[32]

The caste system has forced the masses to slavery by depriving them of the freedom to question — in the name of religion.

Caste in Politics

Caste and power are interrelated in modern Indian politics to a certain extent. The political party based on caste ideology does not fight for the rights and emancipation of the Dalits as such, though they raise their voice now and then against the atrocities the Dalits are suffering.

> Hindus or Muslims were not interested in Dalit's upliftment until the publication of the census reports. After seeing that the Hindus were losing many thousands of Untouchables to other religion, Hindus began to own them. When numbers became politically important, the interest of the Hindu social reformers was further intensified.[33]

---

[31] William Campbell, *British India in its Relations to the Decline of Hindooism and the progress of Christianity* (London: n.p., 1839), p. 162.

[32] Bharat Putra, "Judgment Reserved", Indian Currents, 30 Oct,-Nov. 2006, p. 15.

[33] Das, "Dalits and the Caste System," p. 61.

In a short span of ten years, Kanshi Ram was able to provide a space of their own for Dalit-Bahujans in the politics of the country. His ideology was so clear that it was essential to emancipate the Dalit-Bahujans from the oppressive caste structure, an open war with Caste-Hindus. He had drawn a clear-cut demarcation between the oppressors and the oppressed.

Caste-class and patriarchy, in other words, caste, production and reproduction, have constructed a closed structure to preserve land, wealth and property, women and the ritual quality within it.

> The central factor for the subordination of the upper-caste women was the need to have effective sexual control over such women to maintain not only the patrilineal succession characterizing all patriarchal societies, but also the purity of caste, the system so unique to Hindu society.[34]

Caste Movements and Struggles

The caste system in India was established on the face of this land for grabbing all the resources of this country, opportunities to live and the authority to rule. All movements are the direct consequence of the oppression meted out against the Dalits. Wilson rightly observes, "A sizeable section of the casteless pre-Aryan people lost their proud past, present glory and their very human dignity. They fell victim to a dominant fascist culture and have inherited only untouchability, poverty, oppression and dehumanization."[35]

Caste and British Rule

Bowing to public pressure, the British Government in the 1930s was preparing to give greater participation to Indians in the government of this country.

One of the ways in which this was done was by granting communal representations in the government. "The Scheduled

---

[34] V. Devasahaym, *Frontiers of Dalit Theology* (Madras: Gurukul, 1997), p. 80.

[35] K. Wilson, The Twice Alienated: Culture of Dalit Christians (Hyderabad: Booklinks Corporation, 1982), p. vi.

Castes, then known as the Depressed Classes, were one such group which could take advantage of this new policy."[36]

As a response to the demands from the "untouchable" minority communities in India, the Government of India Act, 1935, redefined:

> The term 'Depressed Classes' as 'Scheduled Castes.' Further, the Government of India (Scheduled Castes) Order, 1936, specified who the Scheduled Castes were. This Order contained a specification that 'no Indian Christian shall be deemed to be a member of a 'Scheduled Caste.'[37]

Though the introduction of the above-mentioned specification was tantamount to using a religious criterion in defining Scheduled Castes, this began to lead to many serious consequences.

It was during the British reign that the caste system became more widely practiced and ingrained in Hinduism. The British encouraged the practice of it to increase divisions between people, thus making it easier for the British to rule over them. A disunited society will hardly have the force and cooperation to defend itself from intruders. Therefore, the British fuelled casteism and kept it more ingrained in society for their own interests.

> In this way, it was many years before the British could be removed. In fact, the British justified their presence with promises of helping keep the peace between the growing divisions in the Indian social structure. In any case, well after the British left, the divisions and the focus on ethnic classifications that had increased during their reign have remained.[38]

With regard to Dalits, it made a special arrangement whereby they would not be separated from the Hindu community on the one hand and yet have their own elected representatives on the other. "Dalits eligible to vote in the general constituency and then in certain selected areas where

---

[36] Jose Kananaikil, *Scheduled Castes in Search of Justice* (New Delhi: Indian Social Institute, 1986), p.1.

[37] *Ibid.*

[38] Knapp, "Casteism' in http://www.stephen-knapp.com

they were most numerous, vote again in 71 separate constituencies of their own."[39]

> The British Government first took up the cause of the Brahmins who suffered tremendously by the change of Government. For enlivening their hearts, the Bombay Government began to educate them in order to enable them to be useful in the service of the new Government.[40]

The position of the Dalits under the British did not improve much. The British authorities took little or no interest in the lives of the slave communities. It was only when the problem of slavery was taken up in England that the British authorities in India were forced to act. "As a result of the anti-slavery movement spearheaded by the Evangelicals in England, the Government of India enacted the Slavery Abolition Act V of 1843 which was followed by the Indian Penal Code in 1861."[41]

During the British period, a number of events took place, which finally led to achieve our freedom from them in 1947. As far as the social practices were concerned, the Britishers maintained the status quo and followed a policy of non-interference, "actively upholding and supporting the caste order."[42]

The rigid communal categories the British and other constitution makers used could not do justice to the complex realities of the Dalit Christians' situation.

Social Reform Movements

All over the world, from time immemorial, different people groups have been experiencing a variety of social reform movements of wide-ranging forms, purposes and methods.

---

[39] John C. B. Webster, *The Dalit Christians: A History* (Delhi, ISPCK, 1992), p. 97.

[40] Report of the Board of Education for the year 1840-1841, p. 24.

[41] Benedicte Hjejile, *Slavery and Agricultural Bondage in South India in the Nineteenth Century* (Copenhagen, n.p.), p. 98.

[42] James Massey, "Historical Roots," in James Massey (ed.) *Indigenous People: Dalits – Dalit Issues in Today's Theological Debate* (Delhi: ISPCK, 1994), p. 33.

Even in India, there are many social reform movements to work for the cause of liberating the Dalits in various ways. There are NGOs and social workers across the country who have been working with the poor and the marginalised people for years. There are liberation movements emerging in many parts of the country. The most significant developments are the Dalits' sharing of power with other political parties in Uttar Pradesh, the most populous state, and the unification of different factions of the Republican Party in Maharashtra. There is decreasing willingness on the part of the Dalits to put up with discrimination at the village level.

Earlier Reform Movements

Some of the movements in Hinduism have welcomed the Dalits into their fold, the earliest being the Bhakti movements of the medieval period. In the 19th Century, the Brahmo Samaj under Ram Mohan Roy actively campaigned against untouchability. The Arya Samaj founded by Swami Dayanand also renounced discrimination against the Dalits. Sri Ramakrishna Paramahamsa founded the Ramakrishna Mission that participated in the emancipation of the Dalits. Upper-caste Hindus, such as Mannathu Padmanabhan also participated in movements to abolish untouchability against the Dalits, opening his family temple for the Dalits to worship. While there always have been places for the Dalits to worship, the first "upper-caste" temple to openly welcome the Dalits into their fold was the Laxminarayan Temple in Wardha in the year 1928. In addition, the Satnami movement was founded by Guru Ghasidas, a Dalit himself. Other reformers, such as Jyotirao Phule, also worked for the emancipation of the Dalits. Ayyankali was a prominent figure in the Dalit emancipation struggle in Kerala in the early 20th century. Another example of Dalit emancipation was the Temple-Entry Proclamation issued by the last Maharaja of Travancore in the Indian state of Kerala in the year 1936.

The Maharaja proclaimed that "outcastes should not be denied the consolations and the solace of the Hindu faith."[43]

Even today, the Sri Padmanabhaswamy temple, which first welcomed the Dalits in Kerala, is revered by the Dalit Hindu community. The 1930s saw key struggles between Mahatma Gandhi and B. R. Ambedkar, most notably over whether the Dalits would have separate electorates or joint electorates with reserved seats. The Indian National Congress was the only national organisation with a large Dalit following, but Gandhi failed to gain their commitment. Gandhi, however, continued to spread his cause for uplifting the Dalits and began the Harijan Yatra. Similar padyatras borrowing from Gandhi's example were established to uplift the Harijans, including Vishwesha Tirtha Swamiji's Padayatras in Bangalore. The Pradeshika Harijan Sevak Sangha, which was Gandhi's organisation, aimed at working on uplifting the backward castes.[44]

Modern Reform Movements

After Independence, many movements sprang up to protect the rights of the Dalits and fight for their dignity. There were social reform movements established to affirm equal rights for all people and equal status for all people.

The Dalit Movement

The modern Dalit movement traces its origins to the 19th century, when Dalits began to make concerted efforts to change their lives and Dalit aspirations began to be taken seriously. Most of the source materials for the background and early history of the movement were written not by the Dalits themselves but by foreigners who became interested in them. The works of these foreign authors, for all their inadequacies, do provide valuable descriptive detail and even statistical compilations that offer a firmer basis for

---

[43] Kuruvila "Dalit Theology: An Indian Christian Attempt to Give Voice to the Voiceless."

[44] *Ibid.*

understanding Dalit history than do the sources the ancients left behind.

Rural Education for Development Society

Rural Education for Development Society (REDS) was started by M. C. Raj in Tumkur district of Karnataka in 1984. It came as a beacon of hope for the Dalits. It aims at protesting against all injustice to the Dalit people. It works for the development of the poor, of the Dalits, especially of Dalit women.

As REDS was an NGO, it was not possible for it to bring about the kind of changes it wanted to bring about. They could not engage vigorously in struggles, in protests and in revolution. They also educated the Dalits and made them realise that their liberation had to come through their leadership. Now the Dalits who live in and around Tumkur came out of their shell. REDS gave them the knowledge they needed to know about themselves. Through REDS, the Dalits gained a political bargaining power and continuously struggled for temple and hotel entry.

The Dalitstan Movement

One of the powerful social reform movements is Dalitstan. This is an all-encompassing country. The country will be governed by the worldview, values systems and economic, political, social and cultural systems of the Dalits. All will have the freedom to be governed according to the principles of Dalitology.

Through the cumulative effect of all the efforts of the ancestors and contemporary leaders, the Dalits wanted to turn India into Dalitstan. The Dalits were not asking for a separate state for the Dalits. The whole of India was their country. They were scattered all over South Asia. According to the Dalitstan opinion, the Brahmins as a caste are responsible for bringing such ignominy on the indigenous people of the country that Dalits were enslaved. They are also responsible for establishing the caste system as a social order that governs the systems of the country.

The Brahmins would be forced to tender a public apology to the Dalit people for making them untouchables, for establishing the caste system as a social order in the name of religion and for all the atrocities that they perpetrated on the Dalit people by themselves directly as well as through the backward-caste people. Manusmriti, which is the codification of an unequal order, must be given up.[45]

Dalitstan focuses on the guard against the fundamentalist tendencies of the dominant Brahminic paradigms of governance. People will have the freedom to govern themselves internally according to their own history, culture and tradition. Even the Dalit Panchayat will have the freedom to write for themselves the principles of internal governance in this model. Each community will have the freedom to distribute values, which means material and spiritual values within the community. They will have the freedom to collect revenues to meet the expenses and governance needs of the community without necessarily having to depend on the State.

The Supreme Council of Dalitstan will comprise of community leaders of all the communities living in Dalitstan. However, the safeguarding of life, dignity and equality of all people is the essence of Dalitstan and it will be given special attention. The group of Dalit leaders will be the guiding principles of the governance of the country. Political governance will be guided by the norms of Communitarian Democracy.

Communitarian Democracy must reverse the history of land grabbing by the dominant caste, class and race all over India. In Dalitstan, the Supreme Council will recognise the labour of the Dalit people as a national resource and enough protective measures will be brought into legislation. It will enact appropriate laws, instruments and mechanisms for the implementation of equal wages for equal work. There will

---

[45] M. C. Raj & Jyothi Raj, *Dalitology* (Bangalore: NESA, 2001), p. 646.

not be any discrimination in the name of gender.[46] In Dalitstan, strict community discipline should be ensured till the dignity of all people is restored.

National Campaign on Dalit Human Rights

National Campaign on Dalit Human Rights (NCDHR) is a national body for the advocacy and lobbying for Dalit human rights. Ambedkar internationalised the Dalit issue by taking it to England and other countries in the world. Since then, there have been sporadic instances of people taking up the atrocities on the Dalits in the U. N. However, such attempts did not find the light of day in the dominant caste-controlled Indian media. Development organisations and movements brought to sharp focus in the UN the issue of caste discrimination in India as a hidden form of apartheid and pressurised the UN to include caste discrimination in Article 1 of the Convention on Elimination of Racial Discrimination, CERD.

Dalit and Minority International Forum

The Dalit and Minority International Forum organises global conferences to discuss the problems of the Dalits and minorities in India. Its chairman, Ram Vilas Paswan, promotes interaction and cooperation among various Dalit and minority groups, which constitute more than 40 per cent of the population of India and to strengthen their cause of justice and equality. The Forum works to give support for the conference and discuss issues confronting them.

Ram Vilas Paswan said, "The Forum is of the firm view that only forces of secularism and social justice can fight communalism, and all Dalits, minorities and weaker sections should unite against the menace as they are the most vulnerable groups."[47] Though this Forum has political

---

[46] *Ibid.,* p. 655.

[47] Ram Vilas Paswan, "Dalit Forum", *The Hindu*, December 28, 2007, p. 13.

connections, it fights for the rights and privileges meant for the Dalits in India.

Mahila Sanghas

There are various Mahila Sanghas established to enable the downtrodden Dalits to stand on their own feet and to live a dignified life. These Sanghas are chalking out a new destiny for the Dalits and their children with help from support groups.

Summary

The patriarchal caste-class structure came into being early in Indian history and has shaped the social ideology of the Indian people, particularly of the Savarnas, groups belonging to the fourfold varna system, and in general, of the Avarnas, the excluded and exterior groups, beyond the four varanas.

Popular social reform movements in India today play a leading role in the liberation struggle of various oppressed people groups. In the current Indian context, the political power of the State is being challenged more by such popular movements than by political parties. Instead of trying to take political power directly, they work to create a powerful social base that has the potential of creating a new society. The creation of a new, participatory power is a major contribution of these social reform movements towards the betterment of Indian society.

Chapter 2

History of the Dalits as the Fifth Caste

Introduction

This chapter deals with the history of the Dalits as the fifth caste in the social hierarchy of the Indian system, explaining their real life-situation and both the secular and church response to that situation. This chapter includes the experiences of some of the non-Dalit intellectuals who have been involved in the process of conscientisation and building up movement of the oppressed Dalits.

Dalit Roots

The term "Dalit" is often used in Sanskrit as a noun and an adjective. The Dalits are continuously denied of their past and so reconstructing the history of the Dalits helps us to draw some conclusions about their roots. Ruth Manorama rightly observes that "the Caste System is probably the longest surviving hierarchical system in existence in the world today; its roots can be traced back to the Manusmriti, a sacred document of the Hindus dating back to the period between 200 B.C. and 100 B.C."[1]

Origin of the Dalits

Even under the best conditions, the question of origins can be a very sensitive matter. For groups, as for individuals, roots, identity, self-image and public image are closely intertwined. Who were the ancestors of today's Dalits? How

---

[1] Ruth Manorama, "Dalit Women: Downtrodden among the Downtrodden," in James Massey (ed.) *Indigenous People: Dalits – Dalit Issues in Today's Theological Debate* (Delhi: ISPCK, 1994), p. 159.

and why did they become untouchables?" Such questions are not purely academic. Answers to such questions can grant or deny considerable psychological and potential power to the Dalits or to their castes.

> The origin of caste lies deep in India's ancient past and the evidence of that origin provided by the archaeological and literary sources now available are circumstantial. The dominant view traces the origins both of caste and of untouchability to the Aryans themselves and to their ways of relating to the peoples of India with whom they came into contact.[2]

The Dalits, called the Dasyas, were the natives of the soil whose towns and fortresses were captured and properties seized by the aggressive Aryans and who were gradually being pushed away from their own villages and towns. They were a different race of people, evidently natives of the soils. It is commonly believed that the Aryans came from outside India.

After some 4,000 years of the Aryan invasion, the original inhabitants of India managed to stand on their own as a distinct people; however, divided with subgroups and ethnic conflicts among them, as they are listed in the Republican Constitution of India as "Scheduled Castes and Scheduled Tribes." The original Indians were counted out as out-castes and as untouchables outside the pale of society, thus calling them a "panchamas" or the Fifth People. It is this fifth people who are today's Dalits. Now they live in every one of the six-lakh villages divided into the two sets of societies as Adi-societies living in the so-called Harijan colonies and away from the main part of the village comprising the Jati societies. Such is the basic division at the village level between the Adi-societies and Jati societies that makes our national polity. There are around 300 million people in today's India who are regarded as the Dalits; they form the bottom base of the social pyramid, with no staircase between the bottom stratum and the other strata of Indian society. They were

---

[2] Webster, *The Dalit Christians*, p. 2.

made to believe that their being outside the pale of Hindu culture and the concomitant misery they experienced were solely due to "fate and karma" and so they had to get reconciled with the status quo. In this way, the idea of revolt was ironed out even at the very beginning.[3]

Names of the Dalits

> Prior to the name Dalit, they are called by various insignificant names. They were called by different names in different parts of the country. Desa, Desyu, Rakshas, Asura, Antyaja, Avarna, Nisada, Panchama, Mletcha, Gapachas, Chandals, and Achuta were the names prevalent as common names for the Dalits.[4]

Brahminism has succeeded in legitimising prostitution by taking it to the temple through the Devadashi system. Devadasis are generally Dalit women. When the question of representation and identification came up for discussion during the British rule, the Dalit people had to be given an identity. Narasimha Mehta identified the Dalit people as *Harijan. Jan* means people. *Hari* is one of the trinity of Brahminism. *Harijan* means the people of god. It is a high-sounding word. But the real meaning is different from what it sounds like. The meaning is that Dalit children are born out of temple prostitution, the Devadasi system. They do not know the name of their fathers. Nor will the mothers be able to remember the name of the true father as many Brahmins, Kshatriyas, Vaishyas and others prostitute the Dalit women in the temple. Since these children are born out of the sexual act that takes place in the temple, since they do not know to which caste they belong and since they do not have a caste, they should be regarded as children of god or *Harijan*. It was in this highly derisive meaning that this name was given to the Dalit people. It was an attempt to rub salt into injury.

> Its common use, the term Dalit today is specially being used for those people who, on the basis of caste distinction, have been

---

[3] G.P. Pitman, *Village India* (London: Marshal, 1951), p. 53.

[4] Aruldoss, *Why Dalit Theology?*, p. 2.

> considered 'outcaste.' They were 'outcaste', because they were not according to the architect of the system fit to be included in the fourfold graded caste structure of the society.[5]

Gandhiji proposed the name Harijan for the Dalits. He praised Dalits as people who live for others and therefore friends of God, who could be rightly called children of God, Harijan.

Many conscientised Dalits protested against and resented the new name because the term *Harijan* had been already used by Mehta to refer to the children of temple prostitutes, children with anonymous paternity. Dr. B. R. Ambedkar, the champion of Dalits, joined in the protest. He said the proposal was aimed at the concealment of a fraud entitling Hindus to a false absolution. When the new name was proposed, nearly all temples had been long closed to the Dalits. They are called children of God without the right to enter into the House of God.

Ambedkar preferred the use of the term "untouchable" as an epitome of Dalit ills and sufferings. He said it was good to call wrong by its name, and that is good for both the wrongdoer and the victim. He said that the new name was indicative of pity and in fact was a ploy to integrate Dalits into Hinduism. "He demanded that the Dalits should have the right to name themselves, which was actualized much later in the Seventies. Ambedkarites in Maharastra popularized the term Dalit as the sign of self-affirmation, self-pride and as a sign of the new identity."[6]

But the educated and enlightened Dalits began to think of their age-old bondedness and lowly position and became conscious of their dehumanised status. They thought of their past identity and lack of self-respect and woke up to fight for their liberation.

> Consequently, they discarded all the contemptuous names and sought a new and approximate name as an expression of their

---

[5] Massey, "Historical Roots," p. 6.

[6] Devasahayam, *Frontiers of Dalit Theology*, p. 13.

> identity. 'Dalit' was the name which met their requirements and
> after 1970s this name came to be applied openly by the Dalits. This
> is the name given by the Dalits themselves, which replaces all the
> unpleasant and insulting names applied by the high-caste people.[7]

The basic meaning of the term Dalit is not poor or outcast;
it really denotes the state to which a certain section of the
people have been reduced through a systematic religious
process and now they are forced to continue to live in that
predicament.

The Dalits are outcast and poor, because they are,
according to the architect of the system, cannot be fit to be
included in the fourfold graded caste structure of our society.
Based on this status, they were made to bear "extreme
kinds of disabilities in the form of oppression for centuries,
which made them almost lose their humanness and finally
they reached the state of being a 'no- people'."[8] The word
"Dalit(a)" comes from the Indo-Aryan root *dal*, and means
"held under check", "suppressed" or "crushed", or, in a
looser sense, "oppressed."

Furthermore, in each State, they were called by different
names. They are Pariahs, Pallas and Chakkillyas in Tamil
Nadu, Malas and Madigas in Andhra Pradesh, Holeyas and
Idigas in Karnataka, Pulayas, Cherumans and Ezhavas in
Kerala, Chamars and Pasis in Uttar Pradesh, Valmikis and
Bhangis in Haryana and Punjab and Mahar and Mangh in
Maharashtra. But all these names implied vulgarity and
humiliation because they were coined by the so-called upper-
caste people who used these names to express their hatred
and contempt towards the Dalits.[9]

"Historically the term 'Dalit' that means the 'oppressed'
'broken' people refers to as outcastes, exterior castes,
depressed people groups, untouchables, downtrodden,

---

[7] Aruldoss, *Why Dalit Theology?* p. 4.

[8] Kuruvila "Dalit Theology: An Indian Christian Attempt to Give Voice to
the Voiceless.

[9] Aruldoss, *Why Dalit Theology?* pp. 2-3.

Harijan and Scheduled Castes"[10]These are the most common labels attached to this term.

> The Dalits especially B. R. Ambedkar discarded the name 'Scheduled Caste' but preferred to be called as 'Untouchables.' Similarly, they rejected the name 'Harijan.' Although Gandhi called the Dalits as Harijan, which means 'Children of God', the Dalits refused to accept it because they considered it as an attempt to appease them by way of giving them a sweet name. Another reason to reject the name is that it means 'Bastard' that is the 'children of unknown father', in other words the children of *Devadasis*[11] born to various priests or godmen.

The Dalits refused to accept this appellation because it was a humiliating and insulting name for them as it estimates them as children who did not know their fathers. Another reason is that the name "Harijan" is not derived from the Supreme Being 'Brahma' but from the inferior deity "Hari."[12]

> The name 'Dalit' is pregnant in meaning. It is an umbrella term under which all the aspirations of the Dalits joined together. It is the name which implies the symbol of change and revolution. The Dalits used this name to regain their past and lost identity. It is also a reminder to kindle their inner spirit in order to revolt against their deprivation and dehumanization.[13]

Divisions of the Dalit Caste

The Dalits are a heterogeneous group in India. There is considerable diversity among them, due either to differences in *jati* traditions and occupations or to variations in regional patterns of landholding and caste interaction. The interaction among Dalit *jatis* is affected by the same considerations of hierarchy that governed all Dalit relations with the higher caste.

The Chuhras, the Chamars, the Mahars and the Paraiyar were among the largest Dalit jatis in modern India. The

---

[10] People or children of God.

[11] Devadasis refers to a system of prostitution for which best-looking girls were dedicated to god.

[12] Aruldoss, *Why Dalit Theology?*, pp. 3-4.

[13] *Ibid.,* p. 4.

Chuhras are not the only scavenger jati; there were the Bhangis in U.P. and Mehtars in Western India. Corresponding to the Chamars in the North were other large jatis engaged in leather work, the Mochis in the Western India, the Madigas in central India, and the Chakkiliyan in the South India. Contemporary observers compared the Mahars to the Dheds in the North as well to the Holayas in what is today Karnataka. The Malas in Andhra Pradesh were said to be Paraiyar by a different name, while in present-day Kerala, the Cherumar and the Pulaya were their local equivalents.

In the context of traditional Hindu society, Dalit status has often been historically associated with occupations regarded as ritually impure, such as any occupation involving killing, handling of animal cadavers or night soil, that is, human faeces. One million Dalits work as manual scavengers, cleaning latrines and sewers by hand and clearing away dead animals. Engaging in such activities was considered to be polluting to the individual who performed them, and this pollution was considered to be "contagious." As a result, Dalits were commonly banned and segregated from full participation in Hindu social life. They could not enter the premises of a temple or a school and stayed outside the village, while elaborate precautions were sometimes observed to prevent incidental contact between the Dalits and the other Hindus.

An estimated 40 million people in India, most of them Dalits, are bonded workers, many working in slave-like conditions to pay off debts that were incurred generations ago. A majority of Dalits live in segregation and experience violence, murder, rape and atrocities to the scale of 110,000 registered cases a year according to 2005 statistics. No one believes these numbers are anywhere close to the reality of crimes committed against the Dalits. Most crimes go unreported, and the few registered cases ever get to trial.

Historically, there may not have been clear demarcation between Dalit castes and the Shudra castes. Dalits are not a single identifiable race or caste. Instead, like the rest of the Hindu society, they are divided into various sub-castes known as "jatis."

A study found some association between caste status and Y-chromosomal genetic markers, seeming to indicate a more European lineage of the higher castes. However, there have been other studies done to indicate no racial and genetic differences between the upper and lower castes. Many sociologists, anthropologists and historians have rejected the racial origins and racial emphasis of caste and consider the idea to be one that has political undertones. Sociologist Andre Béteille, who writes that treating caste as a form of racism is "politically mischievous" and worse, "scientifically nonsense" since there is no discernible difference in the racial characteristics between Brahmins and Scheduled Castes such as the jatav. He writes that "every social group cannot be regarded as a race simply because we want to protect it against prejudice and discrimination."

Dalit diversity may be due to newly outcast individuals or communities. It is noteworthy that the regional tribes that are considered Dalits are sometimes seen by Indians as ethnically distinct. In both northern and southern India, it is different. For example, in North India, in places such as Rajasthan, they are usually lighter because Rajasthan was invaded several times by light-skinned tribes. In addition, they also have different colour of eyes and sometimes hair.

Many Dalits who have converted to other religions in the past few centuries continue to retain their Dalit heritage. In the 1991 census, Dalits numbered just over 130 million and constituted more than 16 per cent of India's population, Discrimination against the Dalits is not limited to the Hindu community. This situation is exacerbated by the fact that non-Hindu Dalit groups have traditionally not been recognised as Scheduled Castes under hiring quota laws. The Dalit Muslims or *Arzal*, as well as Dalit Christians, form an integral part of the caste system in South Asia among

Muslims and Christians. Many Dalit Muslims are discriminated against by the upper-caste *Ashraf* Muslims, and Dalit Christians discriminated against by upper-caste Christian priests and nuns. Dalits and similar groups are also found in Nepal, Pakistan and Bangladesh.

Some Dalits have successfully integrated into urban Indian society, where caste origins are less obvious and less important in public life. In rural India, caste origins are more readily apparent and Dalits remain excluded from local religious life, though this exclusion in its severity is in fact fast diminishing due to changing social norms of acceptable behaviour. Dalits and similar groups are also found in Nepal, Pakistan and Bangladesh. In addition, the Burakumins of Japan are also compared to the Dalits, as are the Baekjeong of Korea.

Muslim Dalits (*Arzal*)

The Muslim society in India can also be separated into several caste-like groups. Descendants of indigenous lower-caste converts are discriminated against by "noble" or "ashraf" Muslims who can trace their descent to Arab, Iranian, or Central-Asian ancestors. There are several groups in India working to emancipate them from upper-caste Muslim discrimination. Dalit Muslims are referred to by the Ashraf and Ajlaf Muslims as *Arzal* or "ritually degraded." They were first recorded in the 1901 census as those "with whom no other Muhammadan would associate, and who are forbidden to enter the mosque or to use the public burial ground." They are relegated to "menial" professions, such as scavenging and carrying. Babasaheb Ambedkar, a renowned Dalit activist and the framer of the Constitution of India, wrote about Dalit Muslims and was extremely critical of their mistreatment by upper-caste Muslims quoting that "within these groups there are castes with social precedence of exactly the same nature as one finds among the Hindus."

In Pakistan, there are estimated to be 6.8 million Mayazurs (bonded labourers) in Punjab and another 7.5 million in Sindh. Although the Pakistani Supreme Court has ruled bonded labour unconstitutional and the National Assembly has passed laws prohibiting it, these laws remain largely unenforced due to the influence of large landlords. Furthermore, the AIBMM is striving to achieve the SC status for India's Dalit Muslims. The lowest in the Muslim communities is a "Muhajir." They are mainly assigned the position of labourer and looked down upon by the Ashraf.

Sikh Dalits

Dalits form a class among the Sikhs who stratify their society according to traditional casteism. The most recent controversy was at village Talhan Gurudwara, near Jalandhar, where arose a dispute between Jatt Sikhs and Ravidasia Sikhs. The different Sikh Dalits are Ravidasia Sikh, Ramdasia Sikh and Mazhabi Sikh. Although Sikhism does not recognise the caste system, many families, especially the ones with immediate cultural ties to India, generally do not marry among different castes.

Christian Dalits

In the Indian state of Goa, mass conversions were conducted by Portuguese missionaries from 16th century onwards. Hindu converts often retained their caste prejudices, attributed to the effectively involuntary nature of mass conversions, sometimes of entire villages. Without conscientious understanding of Christian belief, the existing social stratification was often left unaffected. The Portuguese colonists, despite their violent anti-Hindu iconoclasm, were unable to destroy all aspects of the indigenous culture. Thus, the Dalits who converted to Christianity were still referred to as "Maharas" and "Chambars" (an appellation of the anti-Dalit ethnic slur "Chamaar"). Several ethnic groups who did not convert to Christianity and remained Hindus (such as Marathas) were nevertheless incorporated into the predominately Christian group "Chaddho". Attempts by

Christian missionaries to convert Dalits to Christianity continue.

The Constitution of India guarantees religious freedom and the right to choose one's religion. However, controversies related to mass-conversions have led to laws being passed against such events in some Indian states. Occasionally, Christian converts return to Hinduism after financial rewards some missionaries may have promised as benefits of Christian life are not forthcoming, although there are allegations that some of those conversions are coerced under threats as well.

A 1992 study of Catholics in Tamil Nadu found some Dalit Christians faced segregated churches, cemeteries, services and even processions. Despite Christian teachings, these Dalits also faced economic and social hardships due to discrimination by upper-caste priests and nuns. Other sources support these conclusions, including Christian advocacy groups for Dalits.

Dalits and Neo-Buddhism

There was a mass conversion of Hindus to Buddhism in background. In Maharashtra, Uttar Pradesh and a few other regions, the Dalits have come under the influence of the neo-Buddhist movement initiated by Ambedkar. Some of them have come under the influence of the Neo-Buddhist and Christian Missionaries and have converted away from Hinduism into religions such as Christianity and Buddhism in what they have been told is an "attempt to eliminate the prejudice they face."

In the once-officially Hindu country of Nepal, Dalits and other populations are turning to Buddhism from Vedic Hinduism. The reasons cited are embracing non-violence and a response to the caste system, which has led to a substantial increase in Buddhists in the population, while those professing Hinduism have decreased from 88 per cent in 1961 to 80 per cent and are declining at present.

In the Indian caste system, a Dalit, sometimes called an untouchable or outcast, is a person who, according to traditional Hindu belief, does not have any "varnas." *Varna* refers to the Hindu belief that most humans were supposedly created from different parts of the body of the divinity, Purusha. The part from which a *varna* was supposedly created defines a person's social status with regard to issues such as whom they may marry and which professions they may hold. Dalits fall outside the *varnas* system and have historically been prevented from doing any but the most menial jobs. However, a distinction must be made between lower-caste people and pariahs. Included are leather-workers called *chamar*, carcass handlers called *mahar*, poor farmers and landless labourers, night soil scavengers called *bhangi* or *chura*, street handcrafters, folk artists, street cleaners, dhobi, etc. Traditionally, they were treated as pariahs in South Asian society and isolated in their own communities to the point that even their shadows were avoided by the upper castes.

Discrimination against the Dalits still exists in rural areas in the private sphere, in ritual matters such as access to eating-places and water sources. It has largely disappeared, however, in urban areas and in the public sphere, in rights of movement and access to schools. The earliest rejection of discrimination, at least in spiritual matters, was made as far back as the *Bhagavda Gita*, which says that no person, no matter what, is barred from enlightenment. Buddhist philosophy totally bars discrimination based on caste. There are an estimated 160 million Dalits in India.

Dalit is not a caste name. Dalit is the term used in Western countries for the former "Untouchables" of India. Within India, the National Commission for Scheduled Castes has held that the term Scheduled Caste is the proper constitutional usage for those identified as Dalits in contemporary Western literature. Offensive terms used mostly in the past include *chura, bhangi, neech, kanjjar, mahar* and *mirasi*. Whereas the terms *chura* and *bhangi* are profession-based terms for scavengers; they can serve as general terms for the so-called low-born; others are actual names of the caste. "Harijan" is a term for *untouchable*, which means "Children of God." *Hari* is another name for the god Vishnu. It is now considered patronising (condescending). Calling a person "Harijan" is now a punishable offence in India. Neo-Buddhist Dalits try to make "Harijan" appear as a disgrace to all Dalits as it comes from a Hindu name. This term had already been used in a different form by the medieval philosopher Ramanuja who uplifted many backward caste peoples: as *Thirukulattar* or People of Holy Clan. He was probably the first to allow the untouchables into temples, albeit for limited periods.

Sociological Factors

Dalits are a "No" people made strangers in their own native soil, deprived of their properties as well as their personal human dignity and basic human rights. Dalits are today not allowed to sit on par with dominant castes. They are prohibited to take their marriage processions or ride horses in a dominant caste locality. They are also prohibited from walking with footwear; they are prohibited from carrying dead bodies for burial through the village; tea or coffee is still served in separate glasses, they are prohibited from drawing water even from government sources in the village; temple entry is not allowed; social and economic boycott is being imposed at will; temple prostitution is largely in practice; atrocity on Dalits and raping of Dalit women in work places are common events; atrocities on Dalits take place largely when Dalits participate in democratic processes and make use of police stations.

Dalits cannot enter temples, walk with her slippers on streets dominated by upper-caste Hindus; they are not allowed even to sit on the benches at the local teashops, which still follow the two-tumbler system – glass tumblers for Dalits and steel ones for upper-caste Hindus. In several villages, Dalits are not allowed to sit in government buses if an upper-caste Hindu is around. Upper-caste Hindus cannot accept the fact that a Dalit heads the Panchayat.

Dalits constitute one fourth (16.48 % SCs / 8.08 % STs) of India's total population, which in real terms, comes to 20.25 crores – more than the population of France, UK, and Germany put together. However, as per an independent survey, *In Search of a Dalit Journalist,* The Pioneer, 16 November, 1996, New Delhi, there was not a single Dalit journalist in any of the major media organization in the Capital. This symbolically mirrors the true face of India's caste society.[14]

Social Profile of Dalits

A survey carried out in 565 villages in 12 states, such as "Punjab, Uttar Pradesh, Bihar, Madhya Pradesh, Chhattisgarh, Rajasthan, Maharashtra, Orissa, Andhra Pradesh, Karnataka, Kerala and Tamil Nadu have come out with some major findings which are quite startling":[15]

In 73 per cent of villages, Dalits cannot enter non-Dalit homes.

In 70 per cent of villages, Dalits cannot eat with non-Dalits.

In 64 per cent of villages, Dalits cannot enter common temples.

In 53 per cent of villages, Dalit women suffer ill-treatment by non-Dalit women.

In 38 per cent of villages, Dalit children have to eat separately at schools.

In 33 per cent villages, non-Dalit health workers do not visit Dalit homes.

In 32 per cent villages, Dalits cannot enter police stations.

In 36 per cent of villages, Dalits cannot enter village shops.

In around 43 per cent of villages, Dalits are not denied access to water facilities.

In nearly 70 per cent of villages, Dalits are not required to stand in the presence of a non-Dalit.

As per the census report (1991), of the total landless agricultural labourers in the country, 45.23 per cent are Dalits. That means, almost every second landless agricultural

---

[14] Chandra Bhan Prasad, "Democracy a form of society or a form of governance" (New Delhi: Dalit Shiksha Andolan, 2008), www.dalitchristians.com/html/survey.htm

[15] http://en.wikipedia.org/wiki/Dalit

labourer in the country is a Dalit. Further, to narrate our plight in clearer terms, it will be in order to state that of the total Dalit main work force in the primary sector, 63.54 per cent SCs and 36.32 per cent STs are landless agricultural labourers.[16]

Denial of Access to Basic Services

"In most of the places throughout the country, Dalits are denied access to very basic services."[17] The apathy of officials makes matters worse. About seven lakh complaints are filed every year across the State but most of them go unheard. They fear that things may go wrong if they act tough.

Health

According to National Family Health Survey (NFHS) II data, neo-natal mortality, infant and child mortalities and under-five mortality are higher for Dalits at the all-India level as compared with total mortality for others. Anemia among Dalit Women is more compared to the women of other communities. At the national level, full vaccination among Dalit infants is less compared to others. At the national level, anemia among Dalit children is more than that prevalent among others.

Education

The caste system, which is deep-rooted in Indian society, prevents the Dalits from having an easy access to education. Dalit children are refused either to be admitted to schools or to sit along with high-caste children.[18]

---

[16] Prasad, "Democracy a form of society or a form of governance", www.dalitchristians.com/html/survey.htm

[17] The facts presented here are based on the Report of Sub Group I on an Assessment of the Prevailing Situation in respect of Scheduled Castes and Scheduled Tribes for certain Socio-Economic Indicators, prepared and released by the Office of the Registrar General, Census, Government of India in November 2004.

[18] Aruldoss, *Why Dalit Theology?*, p. 8.

Literacy rates among the Dalits is 45.20 per cent as compared to 54.51 per cent for the total population of India The performance of literacy rates for the Dalits in states like Bihar, Jharkhand and Uttar Pradesh is far below satisfactory, which is below 50 per cent. According to available data, 32 districts in Bihar, Jharkhand and Uttar Pradesh have literacy rates below 30 per cent. The enrolment rate of Dalit students has increased at different levels of education. The drop out rate is still very high—41.5 per cent at the primary level, 59.9 per cent at the upper primary level and 71.9 per cent at the secondary level.

> On the education front, Dalits' position is no better. Of the total Dalit population, 62.59 % SCs and 70.40 % STs are illiterate, and formal education (matric and above) among literate Dalits cannot be more than 8 per cent. The English literacy amongst Dalits must be nominal and computer literacy still a day-dream.[19]

Around 99 per cent of Dalit students go to government schools, where the standard of education is poor. Education is highly privatised. In Jawaharlal Nehru University, Delhi, only 17 per cent of the 22.5 per cent reserved seats were filled. The rest were given to non-Dalits. "In the capital city of Delhi in universities and colleges, the Dalit students are openly called 'shadoos', a derogatory term to indicate beneficiaries of reservation. Their movement within the campus is restricted. In the mess, they have separate tables."[20]

The Sixth All India Educational Survey (NCERT, Vol. III, New Delhi, 1998) has brought out the work force composition of schoolteachers under different management.

> The survey results show that Dalits, SC/ST combined, constitute 17.64 % in the schools run by government, 11.99% in the school run by local bodies, and 9.91% in the schools run by private bodies, which are funded by the State, and a mere 7.07 % in schools run by un-aided private bodies.[21]

---

[19] Prasad, "Democracy a form of society or a form of governance." www.dalitchristians.com/html/survey.htm

[20] *Ibid.*, p. 8.

[21] *Ibid.*, p. 10.

Dalit teachers cannot live in the same area where their "caste" students live. At present, 30 per cent Panchayats practice untouchability and 75 per cent villages do not allow temple entry. Manual scavenging is common in many states. It is being practiced by the state itself.

On the education front, the disparities are rather glaring. In the year 1951, the combined population of SC/Sts was 7.08 crores. By the year 1991, the combined population of SC/ST ILLITERATES was to the tune of 13.29 crores, almost twice the population in 1951.

> As per 1991 census, 62.59 % SCs and 70.40 % STs are illiterates, as against 47.79 % illiteracy amongst non-Dalits. The formal education amongst Dalit literate, education above Matric, cannot be above 7.0 %, English literacy must be negligible, and Computer literacy still a day-dream.[22]

Electricity

According to available data, 44.3 per cent of Dalit households have access to electricity, whereas for others it is 61.4 per cent. Also, 21.4 per cent of Dalit villages have no access to electricity at all, whereas for others it stands at 19.5 per cent.

Drinking Water

Around 27 per cent Dalit households have water sources within premises, whereas for others it stands at 45.2 per cent. Also, 19.5 per cent Dalit households have access to drinking water sources away from their premises, whereas it stands at 14.4 per cent for others. And 32.2 per cent of Dalit households have access to drinking water from tap, whereas for others it stands at 40.1 per cent.

Sanitation

According to available data, 23.7 per cent of Dalit households have access to latrine facility as compared to 42.3 per cent

---

[22] *Ibid.*

Housing

Also, 42.8 per cent of Dalit households have permanent houses in comparison to 57.7 per cent of general households. The condition of housing for Dalits in Orissa, 19.5 per cent; Chhattisgarh, 22.2 per cent; West Bengal, 23.9 per cent; Bihar, 27.9 per cent; Jharkhand, 29.6 per cent; Madhya Pradesh, 34.8 per cent; Uttar Pradesh, 41 per cent; and all the North Eastern States except Mizoram are below the national average.

Poverty

Out of 27.11 per cent of all population living below poverty line in rural areas, the Dalits account for 36.25 per cent. Out of 23.65 per cent of all population living below the poverty line in urban areas, the Dalits account for 38.47 per cent.

About 50 per cent of Dalits still live below the poverty line. Only 30.91 per cent of the Dalits have electricity and only 9.84 per cent of them have sanitation. More than 20 per cent of Dalits do not have access to safe drinking water. Only 37.41 per cent of them are literate. Only 23.75 of Dalit women are literate and 57.5 per cent of Dalit children under 4 years of age are undernourished. "Infant mortality rate among Dalits is 45% more than the national average. 70% of Dalits are denied temple entry and participation in religious processions."[23]

As per the figures provided by the Union Ministry of labour (1996), the total employment in the Government, Central Government, State Governments, Semi-Government, local bodies, organisations is less than two crores, 1.95 crore, and therefore, even if the officially prescribed quota of 22.50 per cent is fulfilled, not even 50 lakhs Dalits stand a chance for an honourable livelihood.

As per the statistics provided by the Directorate of Employment & Training, 1993, there were 63 lakhs Dalits

---

[23] Raj, *Dalitology*, p. 745.

educational achievements/training, waiting on live register for jobs and only a tiny section of them find placement everywhere.[24]

Criminal Justice Administration System

Despite the fact that there are ample laws and regulations to contain the atrocities meted out to the Dalits, the criminal justice administration system has many gaps in the implementation of such legal remedies.

It has been reported that the percentage of acquittals is alarming in the states of Assam, Gujarat, Kerala, Maharashtra, Orissa, Rajasthan, Uttaranchal, Karnataka and Haryana (even to the tune of 97 per cent). The report showed that in theory, from the very moment an atrocity against a Dalit takes place, the road to full judicial remedies and even financial redress through the SC/ST (POA) Act lies open for the victim. But this road is long and has many pitfalls. These data actually relate to the cases that have come to the trial level. When compounded with the fact that less than 5 per cent of the crimes reach the court, the conviction rate is less than 1 per cent.[25]

The Protection of Civil Rights Act 1955 and the Indian Penal Code, in spite of their deterrent penal provisions, have proved inadequate in curbing the atrocities against the members of the SCs and STs, especially offences committed on caste grounds. On August 16, 1989, the Parliament passed another Act — the Scheduled Castes and the Scheduled Tribes (Prevention of Atrocities) Act 1989 — to prevent the commission of offences of atrocities against the members of SCs and STs; to provide for Special Courts for such offences; and for the relief and rehabilitation of the victims of such offences and for matter connected there with or incidental

---

[24] Prasad, "Democracy a form of society or a form of governance." www.dalitchristians.com/html/survey.htm

[25] The Seventh NCSC/ST Report (2001-2002). http://en.wikipedia.org/wiki/Dalit

there to. The President gave his assent to the Act on September 11, 1989, and the Act came into force on January 30, 1990. The term "atrocity" has been defined for the first time in this Act. Provisions have been made for more stringent punishments for committing such offences or atrocities.

The state and union territories have to take specific preventive and punitive measures to protect the SCs and STs from being victimised and where atrocities are committed and to provide adequate relief and assistance to rehabilitate them. There are in all 23 acts that when committed on the members of the SCs and STs by non-SCs and STs constitute an "atrocity" and are punishable under this Act. Although these offences are covered under the Indian Penal Code, the offences under the SCs and STs (POA) "Act 1989 carry heavier punishments than under the IPC. This Act also provides for forfeiture of property, internment and collection of punitive fines."[26]

The cases of atrocities are increasing day by day, but the proportion of acquittal rate is also rising. During the years 1989, 1990 and 1991, a total of 62.38 thousand cases of atrocities committed against the Dalits were reported, in which 2,116 were murdered. These are the cases officially registered at various police stations in the country, and a very high number of cases go unreported.[27]

There are 545 Lok Sabha seats, in which 22.55 per cent seats are reserved for the Dalits, which invariably go to the Dalits because of a clear-cut Constitutional directive. There is no such provision for Rajya Sabha, and so, out of 250 seats, hardly a dozen are filled by Dalit communities. That means that the Indian polity, regulated by the values of

---

[26] *Ibid.,* http://en.wikipedia.org/wiki/Dalit

[27] Prasad, "Democracy a form of society or a form of governance." www.dalitchristians.com/html/survey.htm

varna or caste society, is not at all prepared to accept Constitutional verdicts as the standard-setter.[28]

Historical Attitudes and Discrimination

Traditionally, Dalits were not allowed to let their shadows fall upon a non-Dalit caste member and they were required to sweep the ground where they walked to remove the "contamination" of their footfalls. Dalits were forbidden to worship in temples or draw water from the same wells as caste Hindus and they usually lived in segregated neighbourhoods outside the main village. However, there have been cases of upper-caste Hindus warming the Dalits and Hindu priests, demoted to outcaste ranks, who continued practising the religion. Due to their isolation from the rest of Hindu society, many Dalits continue to debate whether they are "Hindu" or "non-Hindu."

Dalits and Contemporary Indian Politics

In urban areas and some villages, the old concepts of a rigid caste system and untouchability usually no longer exist, though most Indians still voluntarily hold on to their caste origins, which is intended to reflect that their ancestors belonged to their castes with a sense of pride in the duties and responsibilities as required by the caste rules. Another political issue is over the affirmative action measures taken by the government towards the uplift of the Dalits by implementation of quotas in government jobs and university admissions aimed at improving Dalit representation. About 8 per cent of the seats in the National and State Parliaments are reserved for Scheduled Caste and Tribe candidates, a measure sought by B. R. Ambedkar and other Dalit activists in order to ensure that Dalits would obtain a proportionate political voice.

Sociological Traits of Dalits

In India, religion inspires and authorises human collective living. The norms of what constitute human life and who is

---

²⁸ *Ibid.*

part of the human collective emerges from the theological implications of this myth.

According to the Vedas, which is revealed Scripture of the Hindus, "God created the four varnas, i.e., castes, thus the Brahmin from his head, the Kshatriya from his arms, the Vaishya from his thighs, and the Shudra from his feet."[29]

The first of the social traits of Dalits was the harsh fact of social stigma. Dalits were considered polluting and were therefore kept at a distance. Their person, shadow, food and vessels were to be avoided. They were made to live separately and often could not share such common village amenities as the well. The second shared trait of the Dalits was their occupation. No matter what their traditional *jati* occupation may have been, the fact remained that the vast majority of them were actually engaged in agricultural labour of one sort or another. For many their "traditional occupation" was simply a supplementary task over and above their main job of agricultural labour. Their third trait was poverty. The Dalits were very poorly compensated for their labour and so forced to live on the brink of starvation. A few came to own enough land to live comparatively well, while a somewhat greater number left agriculture for the army, the factories, the railways, road gangs, tea plantations and even indentured labour overseas. However, a vast majority faced stark poverty.

The fourth trait was that the Dalits were not part of the *jati* system and that they were organised into *jatis* and functioning like *jatis*. They not only lived and married within their own *jatis*, but also had their own *jati* councils, at least within, if not beyond the local village community. The fifth trait pertains to the complex matter of lifestyle. In many respects, their customs and ceremonies surrounding birth, death and marriage resembled those of the higher castes and Dalit *panchayats* could be as severe as others in enforcing

---

[29] Rig Veda X, 90:11, 12.

caste discipline. To this extent, Dalits shared in a common Indian culture and lifestyle. The other significant trait of the Dalits was that they had little hope of outside sympathy or support. They were suffering a great hardship in the matter of water. They have been the worst sufferers in the exploitative social order. Frequent segregation and exploitation have been their fate. They are born in servitude and die in penury. The National Human Rights Commission concerned with the growing atrocities against the Dalits had this to comment:

> …the atrocities against persons belonging to these groups and the frequency with which they occur is a cause for disquiet. The humiliation which persons belonging to the scheduled castes suffer even today, more than half a century after India proclaimed itself to be a republic is a matter of shame.[30]

Forced Occupation and Manual Scavenging

Some Dalits are confined to undertaking the inhuman practice of manual removal of human excrements from dry toilets with bare hands, brooms or metal scrappers; carrying excrements in baskets to the dumping site—a practice that is prevalent in many parts of India even today.

There are over 1.2 million people engaged in manual scavenging and of these over 95 per cent are Dalits, who are compelled to undertake this inhuman and degrading task under the garb of "traditional occupation." The practice of manual scavenging is illegal and unconstitutional and a blot on the face of humanity.[31]

Bonded and Child Labour

Bonded labour in India, a manifestation of caste and caste-based discrimination, is abolished through Article 23 of the Constitution and the Bonded Labour (System) Abolition Act of 1976. The law mandates the release of all labourers from

---

[30] BBC News Article: *Low-caste Hindus adopt new faith*, Last accessed 15 October 2006.

[31] www.dalitchristians.com/html/survey.htm

bondage, cancellation of their outstanding debts and their economic rehabilitation by the state. There are an estimated 42 million Muslim Dalits and Christian Dalits who count about 16 million. Until a few years ago, they were publicly identified as "untouchables" and are not treated as Scheduled Castes officially, which means they are denied the constitutional safeguards that are available to others who are considered to be Scheduled Castes. "This is a classic case of ways to exclude Dalits from the constitutional safeguards that are guaranteed to other Dalits."[32]

They suffer severe damage and wound in the deepest inner reaches of their soul.

Reality of the Dalits

According to the caste system, as enunciated by Brahminism, the Dalit people do not come under the caste system. They are outside it. They are not recognised as a people. They are still deprived of the right to live and livelihood opportunities. Social and economic justice is increasingly denied to the Dalits and other downtrodden people of society.

Indigenous People

The Dalits and the artisan castes, Most Backward Castes (MBCs), who account for about 60 per cent of India's total population, have been greatly marginalised and are also sandwiched between the upper *varna*-upper *shudra* fight for supremacy.[33]

Ironically, the Dalits themselves have come to believe that they are polluted untouchables, accepting the mud slung upon them by their oppressors.

The definition of indigenous people given by eminent scholars is very much applicable to the Dalits: "There are four major elements in the definition of Indigenous Peoples: pre-existent, i.e., the population is descendant of these

---

32   *Ibid.*

33   *Ibid.*

inhabiting an area prior to the arrival of another population, non-dominance, cultural differences and self-identification as indigenous."[34]

The Dalits have been archaic and backward people for long.

Whether an individual likes it or not, such communications do exist and only through such communications can an individual exist. According to available data, 85 per cent of Dalits live in rural areas and 90 per cent of them are landless labourers. Forcible evictions by dominant castes are common in rural areas. Around 63.14 per cent of rural Dalits are wage labourers. Dalits compose a majority of the 40 million bonded labourers in India. "The primal form of common ideology is the liberation motif of the Indigenous people. They have to liberate themselves form their inferiority complex, from the oppression and discrimination by the dominant people around them in India."[35] Dalits are indeed looking for such liberation.

The first stage, the stage generally ignored by other historians of the Dalit movement, was characterised by mass conversion, especially to Christianity. It is at this opening stage that Dalit Christians made their greatest contribution to the Dalit movement. Their conversions in the hundreds of thousands set the movement going, made the plight of the Dalits a public issue and gave it an urgency that it had previously lacked.

During the second stage, covering the 1920s and 1930s, politics replaced conversion as the movement's dominant characteristic. Since the British set the rules for the political game, this was the politics of numbers between the different

---

[34] Sadruddin Aga Khan and Hassan Bin Total, *Indigenous Peoples* (London: Zed Books Ltd., 1977), p. 6.

[35] Nirmal Minz, "Dalit-Tribal: A Search for Common Ideology," in James Massey (ed.) *Indigenous People: Dalits – Dalit Issues in Today's Theological Debate* (Delhi: ISPCK, 1994), p. 142.

religious communities. The third and present stages, covering the post-Independence period of Indian history, have witnessed the great experiment in "compensatory discrimination" set forth in the Constitution. The history of Dalit Christians, while often a painful story, is nonetheless one in which they can take legitimate pride. They can affirm their heritage and build upon it; they do not have to deny or renounce it in order to live fuller lives in the present. "Picket Waskom reminds us that the Dalits have been reduced to their present state "by centuries of exploitation and servility."[36] The Dalits are the great people of India with human values, who have built this nation with their labour and love for nature. They gave prime importance to women, equated them with divinity and were governing without external interference. The Dalits are people who live in peace and solidarity. They give great honour to elders and women and have lived according to the guidelines of their ancestors.

Historical Evidence for Dalit Reality

Dalits in India are believed to be the ancient *Dravidian* race, the original people of India. We can say that they introduced culture in India. They were the owners of all property. The *Aryans*, a series of related and highly self-conscious tribes sharing a common language and religion, began their invasions of India from the Northwest around 1500 B.C. If a king wins a battle in the neighbouring country, he makes the loser king and his people as slaves and snatches all their properties. Here also, the Aryans snatched away all their properties and kept them aside branding them as outcaste. So, the dominant view traces the origins of both caste and untouchability to the *Aryans* themselves and to their ways of relating to the original peoples of India with whom they came in contact with.

---

[36] Picket J. Waskom, Christian Mass Movements in India (New York: Abingdon, 1933), p. 217.

Untouchability and segregation resulted due to the *Brahmin* supremacy among the Dravidian races. The *Dravidian* race was initially casteless and had horizontal ethnic divisions and clan groups, which under *Brahmanisation* became vertically graded and ritually ranked by the principle of purity-pollution.[37]

According to James Massey, the term "Dalit" is perhaps one of the most ancient terms that have not only survived till date, but are also shared by a few of world's oldest languages, namely Hebrew and Sanskrit. Though they differ in their grammatical and lexicographical connotations, both these languages share the term:

> 'Dalit' with the same root and sense. It has been said that the root word 'dal' in dalit has been borrowed into Sanskrit from Hebrew. The biblical root of the word Dalit is 'dall.' The word 'Dall' is a verb which means to hang down, to be languid, to be weakened, be low, be feeble. Massey also says that almost all English translations of the Bible have rendered these Hebrew expressions with the same meaning and various other translations, including Indian languages have followed the same English sense and meaning.[38]

Elza Tamez, a liberation theologian, while listing the major Hebrew terms used for "poor", has also included *dal*. According to her *dal* is used in two senses: it may refer either to physical weakness or to lowly, insignificant position in the society."[39]

C. U. Wolf, in his essay on the term "poor", which he contributed to the *Interpreter's Dictionary of the Bible*, makes the Hebrew term more clear. For him, "they are those whose prosperity and social status have been reduced. In physical strength and in psychological ability, they are impaired and helpless.[40]

---

[37] Kuruvila "Dalit Theology: An Indian Christian Attempt to Give Voice to the Voiceless."

[38] James A. Massey, "Scheduled Caste: A Special Reference to Scheduled Caste Origin", *Religion and Society* Vol. XXXXVIII, No.3 (March, 1991) pp.30.

[39] Elsa Tamez, *Bible of the Oppressed* (Maryknoll: Orbis Press, 1982), p 30.

[40] C.U. Wolf, "Poor" in *Interpreter's Dictionary of the Bible* (New York: Abingdon Press, 1962), pp. 841-843.

In other words, "dal" or "dalit" people are not only economically or physically poor or weak, they are also poor in their psychological ability and their being has been impaired to such an extent that they have become helpless.

> 'Dalit' in Sanskrit is both noun and adjective. As a noun, dalit can be used for all three genders—masculine, feminine and neuter. It has been accepted in Sanskrit also with root *'Dal'*, which means to crack, split, be broken or torn asunder, trodden down, scattered, crushed or destroyed. Some of the regional languages, including Hindi Dictionaries, have included in the list of meanings, which also refer to a section of people, who have suffered oppression throughout the history because of the accepted religious and social norms.[41]

The term "Dalit" in the Indian context has been used from ancient times, but not very much. Actually, the present usage of this term started since the nineteenth century. "The original usage of this term with its unique meaning was done by Jyotirao Phule of 1827-1890, a renowned backward class social reformer, to describe the untouchable and outcastes as the oppressed and broken victims of Hindu Society."[42]

Thus, "Dalit" can be considered as a title, which the Dalits have given to themselves to describe as people and to denote their real state of deprivation. But it was during the 1970s that the followers of *Dalit Panther Movement* gave currency to the term "Dalit" as a constant reminder of the age-old oppression, denoting both their state of deprivation and as the people who are oppressed.

Today, this term is used frequently and has become popular among the Dalit people of various protest movements of our country. As the uniqueness of the Blacks comes from what has been called the Black condition or Black experience, so also the uniqueness of the Dalits come from their "Dalitness" or Dalit experience.[43]

---

[41] Massey, "Scheduled Caste: A Special Reference to Scheduled Caste Origin", p. 30.

[42] Massey, "Historical Roots," p. 6.

[43] Kuruvila, "Dalit Theology: An Indian Christian Attempt to Give Voice to the Voiceless."

Archaeological Evidence

As far as archaeological evidence is concerned, the story of the origins of the Dalits goes far back in history. The famous sites of these excavations are known as Mohenjodaro and Harappa. Between 1920 and 1951, at Mohenjodaro alone, three foundations, one upon the other, were unearthed. These three foundations indicate that Mohenjodaro had been destroyed more than once. Along with other related areas excavated, it is known as the Indus Valley Civilisation. "Archaeologists have fixed the period of I to III at about 1500 years. The date of the last foundation, Mohenjodaro III, has been fixed around 1500 B.C."[44]

> Destruction of the Indus Valley Civilization and contents of the hymns of the Rig Veda are related. Both these sources point towards a war-conflict amongst different groups of people. This has a direct relationship with the history of Dalits, because the time of war-conflict of these opposing groups will be the beginning of the history of the Dalits.[45]

Archaeological sources are a great help in reaching the historical roots of the Dalits. Archaeological literature has not been written keeping the Dalits in mind but it throws much light on the ancient people of India who could be the Dalits.

Literary Evidence

A distinct literature called Dalit literature has emerged in several regional languages; cultural groups with the aim of retrieving and reviving Dalit culture have attracted innumerable Dalit youth and Dalit community. The story of the roots of the Dalits goes back 3,500 years.[46]

Among the literary sources referred to in this work, the earliest best known is the Rig Veda. "The dates of the

---

[44] Sir Mortiner Wheeler, "The Cambridge History of India, Supplementary Volume," in *The Indus Civilization* (Cambridge: n.p. 1953), p. 86.

[45] Massey, *Roots of Dalit History*, p. 3.

[46] James Massey, "Historical Roots," p. 7.

composition of Rig Veda's hymns also have been put by a number of well-known historians between 1500-100 B.C."[47]

Among the literary sources that throw very clear light on the degraded state of the Dalits is the *Manusmriti*, the Ordinances of Manu, which was possibly composed during the period A.D. 1-A.D. 700.[48]

North Indian Literary Evidence

The Rig-Veda is the earliest written literary source of the ancient history of India. Some of the verses in the Rig-Veda describe how under the command of lord Indra, the Aryas defeated, destroyed, scattered and looted the Dasyas or Dasas. The last two sets of verses indicate the existence of other non-Aryan people with whom also the Aryans waged war.[49] This proves the fact that there were original people who seemed to be the native Indians, the contemporary Dalits.

In the hymns of the Rig-Veda, the main literary source, there are many references to the defeated indigenous groups. Some of the references in this regard are found in 2:20.7, 4.28.4, 6.25.2, 6.69.6 and 7.5.3. The works of Ernest Mackay, H. D. Sankalia and George F. Dales in section 2 (II) hint at the shift or movement of people from Northwest India, Mohenjodaro and Harappa, to other parts of India.[50]

> Manu states that the four varnas were divinely ordained from the very beginning. From the mouth of Purusha, the Self-Existent One, came the Brahmans, from his arms came the Kshatriyas, from his thighs came the Vaishyas, and from his feet came the Sudras. Other castes were the result of alliances between members of these four original varnas. The Candala, whom Manu considered the offspring of a Brahman woman and a Shudra man, the worst possible combination, was to be excluded from all considerations of dharma.[51]

---

[47] Kapur Singh, "Mohenjodaro" in *Pundreek* (Ambala: n.p., 1952), p. 145.

[48] Burneli Arthur Coke (Tr.) *The Ordinances of Manu* (New Delhi: n.p. 1971), p. xxiii.

[49] Massey, *Roots of Dalit History, Christianity*, pp. 10-11.

[50] Massey, "Historical Roots," pp. 52-53.

[51] Excerpts in W. Theodore de Bary, (ed.), *Sources of Indian Tradition* (Delhi 1963), Pp. 225-228.

South Indian Literary Evidence

Most of the literature from South India is much later in date and even more sparse. Current views on the seal characters found in the excavations of the pre-Aryan Indus Valley civilisation are that this is a proto-Dravidian language. This suggests that the people whom the Aryans conquered were Dravidians, who subsequently moved south and subjugated the indigenous people there.

Religion of the Dalits

The Dalits are the original people of the country and their religion is Adi Dharma. They followed different faiths, though many of them considered themselves as part of Hinduism, since they worshipped many of the various Hindu gods and goddesses. The Dalits have gone to other religions in search of equality and dignity. They embraced Christianity and Islam. There were religious and cultural practices in the Dalit community. These have been submerged under Brahminic practices. "The early Dalit culture/religion was animistic-pantheistic, inter-polated by fertility cults and tantric forms of worship, and later on Saivite."[52]

The Dalit religion originated in hot climatic conditions. That is why the worship is conducted during the cool hours and under shady trees, groves and riverbanks. "These aspects clearly show that the Sanskrit religion is a cold-climate religion. This basic difference shows that these two cannot be traditions of one religion."[53]

Christianity has untiringly shown of heaven to the Dalits as something that they should aim for while keeping them in misery on this earth. "The Christian Dalits become concerned not merely with individual salvation, but more with their collective emancipation or liberation. The new

---

[52] Prabhakar, "The Search for a Dalit Theology," p. 208.

[53] James Theophilius Appavoo, "Dalit Religion," in James Massey (ed.) *Indigenous People: Dalits – Dalit Issues in Today's Theological Debate* (Delhi: ISPCK, 1994), p. 115.

religious thrust that is the liberation as salvation becomes the basis of their collective identity and community."[54]

"It is a well-known fact that the majority of Christians come from the lower strata of society, that is, from across the borderline between caste and no-caste. What is missing from Indian Christian theology is the experiences of these lowliest people."[55]

It is also important to remember that in rural areas the converts are often the only members of that religion. So, the question of how their co-religionists accept them is of no importance. What is really important is how they are being treated by the rest of society in that area.[56]

According to various reports and memoranda submitted to various agencies of the Government of India, the caste disabilities suffered by Scheduled Caste converts are in no way different from the disabilities suffered by those who are Hindus. The Christians in various places have separate cemeteries to bury the dead of upper-caste Christians and of the Scheduled Caste Christians, and separate places for worship. "The upper caste Christians will not inter-marry or inter-dine with Christians who are Scheduled Caste converts. These practices have become somewhat mellowed in urban areas, but this is also the case of the Hindu Scheduled Castes."[57]

There are plenty of examples of Scheduled Caste persons converted from Hinduism to other religions reverting to Hinduism in order to take advantage of the benefits.[58]

> The Order is an added insult to the Scheduled Castes themselves, since their freedom to profess the religion of their choice is severely limited by the restrictions of benefits to only those who profess

---

[54] M. E. Prabhakar, "Christology in Dalit Perspective," in V. Devasahayam (ed.), p. 424.

[55] K. C. Abraham, "Emerging Concerns in Third World Theology", *Bangalore Theological Forum* Vol. XXVI, No.3 & 4 (Sept and Dec, 1994) pp. 3-14.

[56] Kananaikil, *Scheduled Castes*, p. 7.

[57] *Ibid.*

[58] *Ibid.*, p. 9.

Hinduism or Sikhism. Given the severe social and economic conditions of the Scheduled Castes, 'this religious criterion forces them to call themselves Hindus or Sikhs even if they are otherwise not interested in the religious beliefs and practices of Hinduism or Sikhism.'[59]

A large majority of the Dalits are Hindus, although some have converted to Buddhism, some to Islam and some to Christianity.

Real Life-condition of the Dalits

Dalits constitute one fourth, 16.48 per cent SCs/8.08 per cent STs, of India's total population. Of the total Dalit population, 77.05 per cent SCs and 90.02 per cent STs are situated in rural India as against 62.17 per cent non-Dalits, who live in the countryside. This means that the Dalits' migration to urban society, one of the indices of development, has been at a much slower rate. Further, of the total Dalit Main Work Force [MWF], 49.06 per cent SCs and 32.69 per cent STs are landless agricultural labourers, as against 19.66 per cent non-Dalits. Interestingly, of the total landless labourers in the country, 7.45 crores, 45.20 per cent are Dalits—almost twice their population composition in the total population of India.[60]

While the Constitution guarantees many rights for the Dalits, the alliance between the dominant caste portion of civil society and the ruling class also guarantees to itself that the constitutional guarantees do not correspond to real life situation of the Dalits in India. "The Indian Reality has grown out of an age-old caste-class culture. Property, wealth, education, social status and political power have been the preserve of upper castes."[61]

A vast majority of the Dalit people are labour-dependent, which means they have been deprived of land as a resource. It is not an accident that the Dalits are left without the

---

[59] *Ibid.,* p. 7.

[60] Prasad, "Democracy a form of society or a form of governance." www.dalitchristians.com/Html/survey.htm

[61] Prabhakar, "The Search for a Dalit Theology," p. 207. pp. 201-213.

resources to live. It is the social system of the dominant castes that has systematically deprived Dalits of their resources.

Dalit Society

The Dalits were kept in a culture of silence for many centuries. They were not able to speak up for their dignity and honour, their rights and justice. "Reservation is given to the Scheduled Castes in order to help them to overcome their extreme socio-economic backwardness. The Scheduled Castes themselves have been trying to use various strategies in order to come up in society."[62]

But none of those strategies has been fully effective. They all seem to have contributed in various ways to bring about some improvement in their condition. It has been there since 1990, but electricity is being passed at night using iron rods for the last 10 days. "The electrification is meant to prevent the Dalits from breaking into the caste Hindu areas during the night."[63] "The next day the Government intervened and consequently the electrified wire was removed. Nevertheless the social suppression continues."[64]

> D. Karthikeyan further reports that the caste Hindus have also thwarted efforts by the Dalits to build a bus shelter. They recently raised the height of a parapet near the bus stop to prevent Dalits from sitting in front of them. Dalits do not visit the teashops owned by caste Hindus. 'They are not allowed to enter streets dominated by a particular upper caste. They are denied space in village squares and community halls and access to burial grounds.'[65]

---

[62] Kananaikil, *Scheduled Castes*, p. 7.

[63] D. Karthikeyan, "Electrified wall divides people on caste lines" *The Hindu*, April 17, 2008, p. 8.

[64] D. Karthikeyan, "The dividing wall remains but loses its electric string" *The Hindu*, April 18, 2008, p. 17.

[65] Karthikeyan, "Electrified wall divides people on caste lines," p. 8.

"Access to common property resources is also being denied to the Dalits."[66] Caste continues to guide social relations in many parts of the country.

Dalit House

The Dalits work hard for long hours yet remain poor. They are poor and are making others rich. They do all kinds of unclean jobs. They take upon themselves the task of keeping others and their environment clean, and in this process, they become unclean and an untouchable people.

Most Dalit women are illiterate and superstitious too. By contrast, Dalit men generally lord it over their women at home, claiming their male prerogatives of being served by their women and dominating their decision-making processes in the family. Female foeticide and child marriages of girl children are common practices among the Dalits.

At home, the Dalit woman is the main breadwinner. She gets up before everybody else in her family gets up and does all household chores, such as cleaning, sweeping, washing, bathing, dressing up children and sending them to school or work and cooking. At dawn, she goes out to work in the fields in her village, sometimes in distant villages. She returns in the evening and does household chores. Often the husband returns heavily boozed and beats her for no rhyme or reason.

At home, Dalit women have to do all household chores. The Dalit male members in the family do not help her with the chores, for they think it is degrading for men to do such work. The result is that the Dalit women have to expect help from other female members of the family and this evokes a quarrelsome response in the family. She also has to forget the very thought of educating her female child.[67]

---

[66] Marimuthu Thonthi, "Electrified wall divides people on caste lines" *The Hindu*, April 17, 2008, p. 8.

[67] Kumud Pawde, "The Position of Dalit Women in Indian Society," in James Massey (ed.) *Indigenous People: Dalits – Dalit Issues in Today's Theological Debate* (Delhi: ISPCK, 1994), pp. 148-149.

The educational, economical, residential and occupational statuses of the Dalits are extremely pathetic. The literacy rate and level of education of the Dalits are very low. Among them, nearly one-third of the males and three-quarters of the females are still illiterates.[68] There is also a correlation between illiteracy and the poverty-stricken condition of the Dalits at home. Dalit parents are poor and so cannot afford to meet all the requirements of school-going children, such as books and other study aids. The poor parents could not nourish their children with balanced diet and as a result, the children are unable to equip themselves intellectually. The Dalits are living in huts with limited space, which is not conducive to their studies. The unemployment situation detours and discourages them from pursing their education. Consequently, Dalit children become ordinary labourers. Although there are educated Dalits, they cannot occupy higher positions due to their poor educational advancement and academic eminence.[69]

The Dalits are the sufferers of the unjust social system and psychologically exploited in society. Still they become a part of that vicious system.[70] They suffer in every aspect of their life in society, though there are some hopeful indications of the fundamental changes in the position of the Dalits due to various government schemes and Constitutional provisions.

The economic condition of the Dalits is also very pitiable. They are the poorest of the poor and nearly 90 per cent of them are living below the poverty line. They live from hand to mouth despite their hard work from dawn to dusk. They are very unfortunate people because they are still struggling for their existence. They lack the basic human needs of food, shelter and clothes and have faced an unending economic crisis for centuries. Their economic backwardness further

---

[68] T. Aruldoss, *Why Dalit Theology?* p. 8.

[69] *Ibid.,* p. 9.

[70] Kumud Pawde, "The Position of Dalit Women", p. 156.

pushes them to various other backward living conditions. Being landless agricultural labourers, they are ruthlessly exploited by their landlords. Most of the Dalits become bonded-labourers and their children are pushed to work as labourers when the parents fail to repay their loans to the landlords.[71]

With regard to their residence, they are set apart from the main dwelling places due to the stigma of casteism. They live in hamlets and are not free from their struggle for shelter, which is one of the basic rights of every human being, particularly in a democratic country like India. The Dalits are either shelterless or live in the most inconvenient huts. Because of poorly housed conditions, they face many predicaments. Owing to their lack of hygienic living conditions, they fall an easy prey to diseases and become vulnerable to all sorts of calamities.[72] Only a very few Dalits are living in good conditions with modern housing facilities.

With regard to occupation, the caste system again plays a key role in fixing up the occupation. The Dalits, being outcastes, have no option to choose their own occupations. They remain agricultural labourers forever and derive their only sustenance from it. Apart from agriculture, they sweep the streets and clean the drains and sewers. Removal of human and animal excreta is also their routine occupation. Since the latrines in their land are not provided with flush, they have to carry buckets of human excreta on their head. Due to their poor educational qualifications, the employment opportunity in the educational institutional is also very low. Due to this, they can improve neither their financial position nor their lifestyle.[73]

The Dalits are backward in almost all occupations, which ultimately smothers upward mobility. Instances of violent

---

[71] Aruldoss, *Why Dalit Theology?*, pp. 9-10.

[72] *Ibid.*, p. 10.

[73] *Ibid.*, p. 11.

clashes between caste and Dalit Christians have also been reported in the Press.[74] In fact, Dalits have been the most degraded, downtrodden, exploited and least educated in Indian society. They have been socially, culturally, economically and politically subjugated and marginalised through three thousand years of history.

Dalit Women

Dalit women are non-violent. There is no history of Dalit women being the exploiters. Nevertheless, they continue to be victims of caste oppression, class exploitation and gender discrimination. They are not only forced to work in the most demeaning of occupations, but also made to suffer sexual exploitation and violence both outside and within their homes. According to the National Family Health Survey-3, more than half of Dalit women face domestic violence.[75] Dalit women cannot affirm themselves as created in the image of God and as subjects of full humanity in a way that diminishes male humanity.

Every day in our country, many Dalit women are being sinned against—in the form of flesh-trade, heavy loads, unjust quotas of work, rape, discrimination in wages, bride-burning, wife-beating and many other forms of harassment, molestation and physical attack. Subhasini Ali, president of AIDWA said, "In Uttar Pradesh, Dalit children are not served but thrown their midday meals, and Dalit teachers are not allowed to make the food for children of higher castes. Even in health centers, Dalit women are discriminated against."[76]

AIDWA feels that the Scheduled Castes and Tribes (Prevention Atrocities) Act that has been put in place to serve as a deterrent against violence against the Dalits is rarely invoked in cases of violence against Dalit women due

---

[74] "Caste in the Indian Church", March 12, 1936), pp. 162-163.

[75] Suhrid Sankar Chattopadhyay, *The Hindu*, 04.11.07, p. 15.

[76] Subhasini Ali, *The Hindu*, 04.11.07, p. 15.

to prejudice of the authorities. It has strongly spoken out against the globalisation policies that are intensifying inequalities and the growth of upper-caste ideology of Hindutva forces, which have adversely affected the rights of Dalit women.

Dalit women are living under the horrific tension of being burnt alive or their husbands and children slain for either violation of eccentric inhuman rules made by upper-caste people or for any other trivial cause. To be a Dalit woman is a great calamity in Indian society.[77]

Though this condition is slowly changing in many parts of South India, it is very much prevalent in rural areas throughout the country.

Dalit women have never really had the courage to challenge the discrimination they face in society. The dilemma of being able to identify the structural forces that dehumanise the Dalit women can be traced to some political thought in India that has not yet been able to fully recognise the specific oppression Dalit women face.

Dalit Women's Identity

The Dalit community keeps woman in the place of mother and adores her. With fraternity as its strong foundation, the Dalit community has always lived together as a community.

The great strength of the Dalit woman is manifest in the magnanimity with which she has faced triple oppression. She has suffered gender oppression as a woman, caste oppression as a Dalit and caste oppression as a Dalit woman. The Dalit community has the capacity to hold people together; especially this capacity is embodied in Dalit women. The liberation of the Dalit community is in the liberation of Dalit women.

---

[77] Pawde, "The Position of Dalit Women in Indian Society," p. 142.

Dalit Women's Rights

The situation of Dalit women is alarming in India. Dalit women have all the capacity, power and potential to govern the world but they are denied the opportunity to realise this potential. In the Hague Conference on Dalit Women's Rights, the first international conference of its kind, Dalit women boldly shared their problems and looked for solutions.

Mary Grey points out:

> Among the many discriminations that Dalit women face, like denial of access to education, meaningful employment, healthy provisions, etc., the worst is violence in many forms (including temple prostitution), they are also frequently raped to humiliate Dalit men, something quite common even today. The degrading work of 'scavenging' also falls mostly on Dalit women, since men are more likely to be 'upward-mobile.'[78]

Dalit women's problem is not of caste alone, but also of a feeling of getting sidelined by men in the Dalit movement itself and even within the women's movement of the country. Despite their problems, a new strength is emerging among Dalit women to challenge caste boundaries, contributing to their self-esteem.

Dalit Women's Situation

The situation of Dalit women is unbearable. An upper-caste man can command the company of a low-caste woman. Dalit women suffer oppressions of patriarchy, caste and class. Violence, female infanticide, prostitution, discrimination and exploitation have been the lot of Dalit women. They suffer illiteracy, poverty, ill health, crude forms of wife-bashing and physical assault. The concerns of Dalit women are ignored by both women's movements and Dalit movements. "A Dalit woman is a downtrodden among downtrodden.

---

[78] Mary Grey, "Dalit Women and the Struggle for Justice in a World of Global Capitalism" in Ranjita Biswas, Society: On the Wings of Dreams, The Hindu, May 13, 2007, p.5.

She suffers in the family, first, because she is a woman and then she has to face the society as she is a Dalit."[79]

> Christian Dalit women, who have a heritage of active participation in the Church and socio-economic activities, are in the forefront of struggles for freedom from oppression. Their simple but deep faith in God and Jesus Christ, their belief in the Bible, their prayerfulness, tenacity and courage, amidst atrocities, braving violation of their bodies and spirits all have significant implications for Dalit solidarity.[80]

"Dalit women in India number 80.517 million or approximately 48% of the total Dalit population, 16% of the total female population and 8% of the total Indian population of the country."[81] Disaggregated data are available on the status of Dalit women's enjoyment of their rights to education, health and work participation, all of which indicate their lower levels of enjoyment of these rights as compared to non-Dalit/Adivasi women and men.

The question of caste discrimination, untouchability and violence has been extensively documented, but mostly with reference to the Dalits as a group and not with specific reference to Dalit women's experiences arising from the intersection of their descent and occupation-based identity with their gender identity.[82]

"The use of Dalit women's caste names in verbal altercations or threats leading up to or following violence is indicative of how Dalit women's caste-and gender identity invites violence towards the women. Violence acts as a crucial social mechanism to maintain Dalit women's subordinate position to particularly dominant caste men.[83]

---

[79] Kumud Pawde, "The Position of Dalit Women," pp. 147-148.

[80] M. E. Prabhakar, "Christology in Dalit Perspective," in V. Devasahayam (ed.), pp. 404-405.

[81] Government of India, *National Census of India 2001*, Final Population Totals, 2004.

[82] *Ibid.*

[83] Report of Prevention of Atrocities against SCs and STs, *National Human Rights Commission*, New Delhi, 2004, p.10.

Moreover, any attempt by Dalit women to assert their fundamental right to equality with dominant castes in any sphere — social, cultural, economic, civil and political — is met with violence, while reinforcement of Dalit women's lack of or denial of access to land and other economic resources through violence points to their effective economic subordination in order to retain them as an exploitable labour force for their dominant caste employers.[84]

Attacks on and threat to Dalit communities and women are on the increase at present. An analysis of 400 rape victims by Platform Against Rape revealed that more than 80 per cent victims belonged to lower-caste Dalits and tribal groups and came from the poor class of society.[85]

Leaders' Response to the Dalit Cause

There are people who stood against various manipulations and exploitations meted out to the Dalits. The secular response to the Dalit cause has been so tremendous that it paved the way for various kinds of reformation in various parts of the country. Some prominent men responded to the cry of the Dalits directly or indirectly.

Mahatma Gandhi

Mahatma Gandhi did speak against the practice of untouchability. He was genuinely against it. He wanted the dominant caste fellows to change their hearts vis-à-vis the Dalit people. Even Gandhi, the acknowledged champion of the Harijan untouchables, had no difficulty with what others called "Varna-Ashrama-Dharma" that is the hierarchical and graded caste system of which the original inhabitants have become victims as outcastes and as the *panchamas* thus pushed to the bottom of society as slaves.

---

[84] *Ibid.*

[85] Ruth Manorama, "Dalit Women: Downtrodden among the Downtrodden", p. 165.

Gandhi was an emancipator of all Indian population under the political subjugation of the British, though he conceded that the problem of Harijan was of a special dimension. He has his own philosophy of life that was predominantly religious.[86]

His fast on September 20, 1932, in Yervada Jail, Poona, was quite dramatic in its impact. Gandhi told the Hindu leaders before he began the fast that he wanted the end of untouchability and not simply a political agreement. Thus, while the leaders negotiated, caste Hindus opened hundreds of temples, wells and other public places to Dalits and sponsored inter-caste meals with them.

Gandhi broadened his protest against what he considered an unacceptable development in the politics of numbers into a crusade for the removal of untouchability. He seems to have argued on the assumption that the so-called untouchables are a part of the Hindu society. Caste-Hindus are mainly responsible for the position of the untouchables.[87]

> Christians were generally supportive of Gandhi's efforts to change Hindu attitude and to remove the disabilities from which Dalits suffered. Gandhi was always against the religious conversion. 'In his view, the Dalits were becoming Christians because of material rewards offered or hoped for, although he did concede that blind rebellion against untouchability was also a factor.'[88]

He also felt that to dignify the current competition for the Harijan religious allegiance with the name of spiritual hunger is a travesty of truth. Gandhi called Ambedkar's rejection of Hinduism "unbelievable, ...especially when untouchability is on its last legs ... Religion is not like a house or cloak which can be changed at will."[89]

---

[86] J. A. David Onesimu, *Dr. Ambedkar's Critique Towards Christian Dalit Liberation* (Delhi: ISPCK, 2008), p. 47.

[87] *Ibid.*, p.51.

[88] M. K. Gandhi, Christian Missions: Their Place in India (Ahmedabad, 1941). p. 92.

[89] Putra, "The Great Conversion," p. 26.

Gandhi even depicted Dalits as mindless followers when he wrote to C.F. Andrews, "The poor Harijan have no mind, no intelligence, no sense of difference between God and not-God."[90] Gandhi had no clue to the mind of the Dalit. He did not know that the Dalits were not blindly following their leader into a new religion. A churning process had been going on all over the country.

Gandhi's contribution to humanity and his legacy are far beyond the scope and limitations of any awards or recognition; humanity would always acknowledge him as the greatest apostle of peace in the modern world.

B. R. Ambedkar

In 1935, Ambedkar, a Hindu Dalit by birth, boldly denounced untouchability and even declared, "I had the misfortune to be born with the stigma of 'untouchable'. But it not my fault, but I will not die a Hindu for this within my power."

"Later the declaration had this effect and most Dalit leaders denounced it. In 1956, he embraced Buddhism as the true alternative to Brahminism. Although Hindu religion, its priests, scriptures and social system imposed utmost injustice upon the depressed classes, Ambedkar did not reject the very concept of religion like Karl Marx."[91]

"Ambedkar firmly believed that a radical change in the structure of Hinduism and in the outlook of the Hindus was necessary, without it there would be no real reform in the Hindu society."[92] "Ambedkar maintained that "untouchability is born out of the struggle for supremacy between Buddhism and Brahmanism."[93]

Ambedkar felt that Gandhi and other caste Hindus had failed in removing untouchability. He sought the emancipation of the Dalit people through the path of religion.

---

90 *Ibid.*

91 Onesimu, *Dr. Ambedkar's Critique*, pp. 19-20.

92 *Ibid.,* p. 11.

93 Keer, *Dr. Ambedkar's Life and Mission*, p. 407.

His Dalit Theology can best be summarised as concepts of liberty, equality and fraternity. But he insists that he had not borrowed these ideas from the French Revolution. His liberty, equality and fraternity are rooted in religion.[94]

According to him, political liberty and political equality were not enough for the Dalits. There must be social freedom and social equality. In India, where society is divided by the *varna* ideology, political democracy must be translated into social democracy. The basic principle of social equality is the dignity of the human person. "The words human, humans and humanity are at the centre of Ambedkar's Dalit philosophy. Only value-based understanding of the human person can promote fraternity."[95]

Ambedkar proposed independent autonomous settlements for the untouchables, "distribution of land to the landless agricultural labourers, nationalization of the land by the state, industrialization and urbanization of the Indian villages."[96]

Ambedkar, a Dalit himself, developed a deeper analysis of untouchability, but lacked a workable political strategy: his conversion to Buddhism in 1956, along with millions of followers, highlighted the failure of his political endeavours. India's first Prime Minister, Jawaharlal Nehru, based on his own relationship with Dalit reformer Amebdkar, also spread information about the dire need to eradicate untouchability for the benefit of the Dalit community.[97]

Ambedkar's life itself is a powerful parable of the truth that God raises the lowly and exalts the downtrodden. He

---

[94] B.R. Ambedkar, Philosophy and Hinduism in Vasant Moon (ed.), Dr. Ambedkar: Writing and Speeches, Vol. 3 (Bombay: Government of Maharashtra, 1987), p. 25.

[95] Onesimu, Ambedkar's Critique, M.Th. Thesis, 1996, p. 76.

[96] *Ibid.*, p. 80.

[97] Kuruvila "Dalit Theology: An Indian Christian Attempt to Give Voice to the Voiceless."

was born in an untouchable family of the Mahar caste. During his childhood, he had to face all the demonic discriminations of the caste society, which takes extraordinary care that no one from the oppressed Dalits goes up the social ladder. He grew up as the enfleshment of God's liberating grace among the Dalits and attained heights of socio-political recognition, which are simply impossible for most of his people. "He dedicated every ounce of his life, his energy and influence for the holistic liberation of all his people."[98]

Ambedkar denounced Christianity not only for failing to uproot casteism among the converts, but also for encouraging it by permitting the converts to practice some of their pagan practices as concession to gain conversion. "He was not that harsh with the Protestant missionaries and their methodology, though he exposed their weakness also in building a casteless Church."[99]

His life provides an example and an inspiration for the downtrodden masses of humanity that no bar of class, no bar of caste, no bar of privilege, no bar of riches, can prevent the full attainment and growth of an individual who is determined to build his personality on patient labour, burning sincerity, supreme courage and selfless sacrifice.

In Ambedkar's view, the caste system is a social division of people of the same race and is not merely a division of labour, but also a division of labourers, compelling a man to engage himself in a calling that may not appeal to him. The caste system deadens, paralyses and cripples the people from helpful activity.[100]

E. V. Ramaswamy Naicker

E. V. Ramaswamy Naicker, popularly known as Periyar, the Great Man, went on a vituperative attack on the Brahminic

---

[98] Keer, *Dr. Ambedkar: Life and Mission*, p. 494.

[99] Ambedkar, "Philosophy of Hinduism," in *Writings and Speeches*, Vol. iii, p. 23.

[100] *Ibid.*, p. 269.

forces in this country. The great nationalist that he was, he fearlessly exposed the shenanigans of Brahminism even to the common people so that in Tamil Nadu, Brahminism was literally on the run.

EVR launched the Dravidian movement known as the self-respect movement. He was not only an anti-Brahmin ideologue, but also a courageous fighter against the evil of Brahminism. He laid the foundational principles of his rationalism as "no god, no religion, no Brahmin, no Gandhi and no Congress." He went out with his army of followers and broke statues of gods and goddesses, fought for temple entry for Untouchables and fought Brahminism tooth and nail on all fronts. He fought for the establishment of political nationalism in India as against the cultural nationalism of the Hindu fundamentalist forces.

EVR started a self-respect movement in 1926 and the Dravidar Kazhagam in 1944. He viewed *swaraj*, that is, self-rule as a conspiracy by the local elite to subdue the lower classes. He called it dishonest on the part of Indians since they were not willing to abolish the oppression of the Dalits and women. He argued that India is not a nation but a museum of castes, religions, languages and gods.[101] EVR remarked, "India is not a country but is a museum of castes and religions. In this museum, people allow dogs that eat shit. But they will not allow inside their home Dalits who have human values."

While Jotiba Phule was the first one in the history of India to open schools for the untouchables, EVR fought tooth and nail against the Brahminic forces of India in the name of the Dravidian Movement he started. He fought Brahminism in his own specific way.

Church's Response to Dalit Cause

One of the most significant facts of the Indian Church is that a vast majority of Christians, from two-thirds to three-

---

¹⁰¹ Raj, *Dalitology*, p. 423.

fourths, is drawn from the Dalit community. Christian Dalits are becoming increasingly aware of the indifference and insensitivity of the Indian Church to the sufferings, struggles and aspirations of over 250 million Dalits in general and of Christian Dalits in particular.

> The Dalit Church with upper-caste leadership and upper-caste theology forgot the social base of the Indian Church. It has accommodated caste system which benefits the caste people, identified with the status quo in terms of social relations among Christians characterized by division, discrimination and domination. It has grossly failed to general a critical social consciousness. Christian Dalits are becoming aware of the inadequacy as well as the gap between church's theology and practice.'[102]

The Dalits were seeking their dignity, self-respect and self-identity as their first and foremost priority. To achieve this goal, they found conversion as one of the ways and means. They therefore embraced other religious faiths such as Christianity, Islam, Sikhism and Buddhism. The waves of mass conversion to different religions have taken place during the 19th century. What is to be noted is that these conversions were mainly for dignity and equality and not for economic benefits as it is generally interpreted.

"With these conversion activities, the Dalits fervently hoped for a new social and religious identity. In other words, they discarded the religion that advocated inequality which was detrimental to their emancipation but embraced other faiths in order to make themselves free from all the unwanted clutches and disabilities."[103]

Unfortunately, conversion to Christianity has in no way helped the Dalits to escape from their age-long discriminations. On the contrary, Christianity accommodated the caste hierarchy and thus added their misery by way of maintaining the inequality as high- and low-born Christians,

---

[102] V. Devasahayam, "Doing Dalit Theology: Basic Assumptions," in V. Devasahayam (ed.), *Frontiers of Dalit Theology* (Delhi: ISPCK, 1997), P. 271.

[103] Aruldoss, *Why Dalit Theology?* pp. 11-12.

which is against the cardinal features of Christianity. "The treatment that the Dalits received inside the Church did not differ from what they got outside the Church."[104]

The dominance of the upper caste in Church administration has been constantly maintained by upper-caste Christians. The leadership control was only with upper-caste Christians at all levels despite nearly 75 per cent of the Christians being Dalits. The Dalits were excluded from decision-making bodies. Most of the job opportunities within Church-run institutions went in favour of upper-caste Christians. Candidates to priesthood were not recruited from among the Dalits.

"Ever since that time, low caste people have accepted baptism more readily than others. Because of caste feeling, Christians of high caste origin were sometimes reluctant to evangelize the low castes or welcome them into their congregations."[105]

The present-day Dalit Christian Theology, unlike its predecessors in the earlier stages of Dalit Christian history, is not evangelistic. It seeks solidarity with, not the conversion of, fellow Dalits. It assumes religious pluralism among the Dalits and draws upon Christian faith to help Christian Dalits in the common struggle for liberation, justice and dignity. It does not try to impart a distinctively Christian vision to other Dalits, but instead speaks more modestly "from faith to faith." "It is a shared ideology, not Christian theology, which provides the basis for united action by Christians and other Dalits."[106]

Missionaries were not in contact with Adi Dravida communities for very long before they realised there was

---

[104] *Ibid.*, pp.12-13.

[105] P. Rajagopal, "Caste in its Relation to the Church", *Indian Evangelical Review*, vol. IV, January 1877, p. 366.

[106] Webster, *The Dalit Christians*, p. 231.

more involved than preaching the gospel and reaping a great harvest of souls. The circumstances of those among whom they found their converts demanded that missionaries give attention to their earthly needs as well.[107]

In this connection, the words of the Editor of the *Indian Currents* journal are very apt: "Even as the much-maligned casteism is ebbing away in Hinduism, it is firming up its hold and spreading its tentacles in the Church in India, especially in States like Tamil Nadu and Andhra Pradesh."[108]

Dalit Christians are forbidden to use the church road, which is the main road in the village. They have to take a separate path to reach their reserved area in the church. Processions in the village have a great social value. It is customary to take out marriage, festival and funeral processions through the main street. Use of this street remains barred for Dalit Christians. The Parish also has a separate cemetery and a hearse. Dalit Christians are not permitted to bring their dead to the church for funeral mass.[109]

The Church's response to the affliction of the Dalits is very crucial and should prove to the world that caste has no place in Christianity and that giving any credence to caste is an aberration of the teachings of Lord Jesus Christ.

> There is no parish, no religious house, no school, no college either run by diocese or Religious Congregation, which can claim to be completely free from the shadow of caste prejudices. Caste considerations play decisive role in appointments and transfers of clergy in parishes; naming of superiors to religious communities and heads of educational institutions; and recruiting staff for institutions.[110]

---

[107] Graham Houghton, *The Impoverishment of Dependency* (Madras: CLS, 1983), p. 101.

[108] Jacob Kani, "Editor's Message" *Indian Currents*, Vol. XX, No. 13-14 2008, p. 5.

[109] Emanuel Savariaradimai, "Caste Ghost Hants Church," *Indian Currents*, Vol. XX, No. 13-14 2008, p.34.

[110] *Ibid.*

"A theology of the Church in the world should be complemented by a theology of the world in the Church." Joining in solidarity with the oppressed against the oppressors is an act of "conversion", and "evangelisation" is announcing God's participation in the human struggle for justice.[111]

"As men of faith, priests must not let the temptation of power or material gain distract them from their vocations, nor can they permit ethnic or caste difference to detract from their fundamental change to spread the Gospel."[112]

"Death and devastation have been the usual answers to the Dalits whenever they raised their voices in quest for their human rights and dignity."[113]

The Church fails to respond and oppose the different discriminatory caste practices as unjust and incompatible with its faith and practice. The following event is an example:

> Demanding an end to all forms of discriminations in the church, the Dalit Christians at Eraiyur boycotted the Palm Sunday liturgy and hoisted black flags in church campuses. In a number of places, they locked up churches and asked the high caste priests to leave. The Dalit Christians; Liberation Movement has given a call to observe the Holy Week as the 'untouchability week.'[114]

The main part facing the altar was reserved for the high castes, the rear portion for the lower castes and Dalits. Some churches had walls or grills to segregate the Christians of different castes. There were separate holy water and baptismal fonts.'[115]

---

[111] Jean-Bertrand Aristide, "Liberation Theology" at http://mb-soft.com/believe/txn/liberati.htm

[112] Pope John Paul II, quoted by Justine Emmanuel, "Living with Ignominy," *Indian Currents*, Vol. XX, No. 13-14 2008, pp. 38-39.

[113] Justine Emmanuel, "Living with Ignominy," *Indian Currents*, Vol. XX, No. 13-14 2008, pp. 38-39.

[114] Emanuel Savariaradimai, "Caste Ghost Haunts Church," *Indian Currents*, Vol. XX, No. 13-14, 2008, p. 35.

[115] *Ibid.*, pp. 34-36.

The government of India is also denying the rights of the Dalit Christians despite the constitutional provision. The government grants privileges and job opportunities to Hindu Dalits but denies the same to Christian Dalits although they live in similar conditions and in abject poverty. This means that the Scheduled Caste status is denied to Dalit Christians only, though Sikhs and Buddhists have been included in the list of Scheduled Caste. The condition of the overwhelming majority of Dalit Christians is equal to that of their Hindu counterparts and they are also in need of liberation and eagerly waiting to get it. "...proclaim (by) word (and) by their own efforts the power that will permit them to guarantee the satisfaction of their needs and the creation of authentic conditions of liberation."[116]

Summary

The Dalits are the descendants of the earliest settlers of India. The history of the Dalit's present problem began around 1500 B.C. and for more than 3,500 years, they have suffered and continue to suffer multiple oppressions. Because of the long history of oppression, the Dalits have even lost their self-identity of full human being, and this in the real sense is the inner captivity of their being from which they need liberation.[117]

The social structure of India is stratified, with inbuilt inequalities and injustices, based on the caste-system sanctified by Brahmanic-Hinduism. The mass-poverty, mass-illiteracy and mass-unemployment are distinctive characteristics of an under-developed society, which, sadly enough, India is, in spite of its ancient heritage of spiritual wisdom, scientific knowledge and remarkable modern progress.[118] Dalits are getting tired of being governed; they

---

[116] Tissa Balasuriya, "Theologizing from the Other Side of the World", *Logos*, Vol. 20, No. 3, Sept. 1981, p. 31.

[117] Massey, *Roots of Dalit History*, p. 53.

[118] Prabhakar, "The Search for a Dalit Theology", p. 207.

are impatient to govern. Dalits have a strong urge for self-determination and self-realisation. These have resulted in an increased violence against the Dalits, yet the liberative ferment seems to be endemic and its effects are felt in the Indian Church.

Chapter 3

Similar Types of Theology

Introduction

The term "theology" has two major aspects. The first aspect is God's eternal self-revelation connoted by *theos*. The other aspect is people's understanding of God in categories of *logos* or reason. The task of theology for any people is to articulate their understanding of the eternal truth in terms of their specific local context. In this sense, there can be various types of theology, such as Western Theology, Third World Liberation Theology, Korean Minjung Theology, theology of the oppressed and Indian Christian Theology. In spite of differences among these theologies, all of them, except for some forms of contemporary theology, attempt to embody the same core of biblical thought.

There are some well-known theological expressions that have not only a common historical base to operate, but also a common goal, namely the liberation of all people. The Latin America-born Liberation Theology, South Africa-born Black Theology, the Korea-born Minjung Theology and the Philippines-born "a theology of struggle" are good examples of the Third World Liberation Theology. These have taken shape from the pain, struggle and oppression of the common people.

Traditional Western Theologies

Traditional Western theologies developed in dialogue with Greek philosophy and flourished for almost two millennia since the employment of the key concept of the latter, logos, as the root-metaphor of theology.

"The goal of theology, primarily as God-talk, is to transmit universal orthodoxy. However, most contemporary theologians claim that this logos phonocentic paradigm is anachronistic and is no longer viable, not to mention criticisms from deconstructionists."[1]

"Western theology means the Western Christian's beliefs and formulations concerning God and man's relationship with Him."[2] It is often perceived as being built on an idealistic conception of truth, which sharply distinguishes it from its practice. This leads to a theology that is "unengaged" and, therefore, lacks the power for human and social transformation.[3]

Western theology is basically abstract and almost a-historical. The six basic sources of western theology are experience, revelation, Scripture, tradition, culture and reason.

The traditional western theology is speculative, *kerygmatic*, logos theology, individualistic, other-worldly and dicthotomic theology that it underestimates social evils. It is said to be pietistic and capitalistic in scope and function.[4]

This is the theology that was operative in the past and is operative today in our churches and elsewhere. The concept of original sin, obedience and personal holiness are the three important aspects of this theology. It is essential to look at other similar theologies to situate the relevance of Dalit Christian Theology.

For Western theology to survive, it must produce a new understanding of faith, which gives emphasis to not only

---

[1] Heup Young Kim,, "A Tao way of Asian Theology in the 21st century: From the perspective of the Ugmchi Phenomen," in Renthy Keitzar (ed.), Journal of Tribal Studies, Vol. IV, No. 2, July-December, 2000. Pp. 52-53.

[2] Billy K. Simbo, "An African Critique of Western Theology," *Evangelical Review of Theology* Vol. 7, Number 1, April 1983, p.28.

[3] Hwa Yung, *Mangoes or Bananas? The Quest for an Authentic Asian Christian Theology* (New Delhi: Oxford, 2000), p. 8.

[4] Franklin J. Balasundaram, "Dalit Theology and other Theologies," in V. Devasahayam (ed.), *Frontiers of Dalit Theology)*, Delhi: ISPCK: 1997), p. 252.

philosophising and theologising but also to faith that can be translated into lifestyles.

Western Paradox of Either/Or

One of the characteristics of Traditional Western Theology is the use of the either/or thought pattern of Greek philosophy. Henceforth the dualistic pattern of "either/or" has been well entrenched in the Western mind. This "either/or" pattern has several variations: the dualistic cosmology of ancient Greece, the dialectics of Hegel, i.e., "dialectic idealism, Marx, i.e., dialectic materialism, and Augustine, i.e., dialectic sociology of the Kingdom of God and the Kingdom of Man."[5]

Great thinkers of the Western tradition have been forced to follow the path of the either/or thought pattern for too long. The table given below gives examples of the dualistic thought pattern.

TOPIC	EITHER	OR
Christology	<u>Either</u> the deity of Christ	<u>or</u> the humanity of Christ
	<u>Either</u> the Christ of <u>kerygma</u>	<u>or</u> the historical Jesus
Soteriology	<u>Either</u> God's sovereignty	<u>or</u> human free will
	<u>Either</u> faith	<u>or</u> reason
	<u>Either</u> grace	<u>or</u> work
	<u>Either</u> evangelism for conversion	<u>or</u> social gospel as witness
Ecclesiology	<u>Either</u> the universal church	<u>or</u> local congregation
	<u>Either</u> organic unity	<u>or</u> organisational uniformity
Eschatology	<u>Either</u> already realised	<u>or</u> yet to come
Bibliology	<u>Either</u> divine revelation	<u>or</u> human authorship

---

[5] Enoch Wan, "Critiquing the Method of Traditional Western Theology and Calling for Sino-Theology," 1998.

Traditionally, Western theology has been characterised by its systematic approach to the subject. The greatest Western theologians have been systematic theologians.

"The main characteristic of the systematic theologian is that he begins his theologizing with theological categories like God, Christ, the Holy Spirit, the Church, etc., and attempts to have a systematic presentation of the doctrines of the Christian faith."[6]

The first several hundred years of the Christian church were known for the Christological controversies due to the either/or perspective on the nature of Christ. This debate has been revised in the last few decades by biblical scholars in the New Testament studies of the "historical Jesus" as a response to the neo-orthodox insistence on the "Kerygmatic Christ".[7]

> The 'fundamentalist movement' of the early part of the 20th century was mostly a struggle to proclaim and practice evangelism as a matter of personal and spiritual conversion, fighting first against the 'social gospel' of the liberal, and later against 'institutional salvation' of World Council of Church and liberation/feminist theology. The underlying assumption is that salvation is either a spiritual/personal matter or an institutional/collective matter.[8]

This traditional Western theology is a part of our Christian heritage. Theologians should attempt to provide correction to it as well as reinterpret the tradition in our particular context.

Third World Liberation Theology

Until recently, the dominant theologies in the Third World were Western. These failed to speak to the specific context of Third World Christianity. During the last four decades or so, however, various indigenous theologies have emerged

---

[6] Ismael E. Amaya, "A Latin American Critique of Western Theology," *Evangelical Review of Theology* Vol. 7, Number 1, April 1983, p.13.

[7] Wan, "Critiquing the Method of Traditional Western Theology and Calling for Sino-Theology."

[8] *Ibid.*

in the Third World. They have begun to make a significant contribution to the theology of Christendom at large.

The social and cultural context in which the Bible was written is very similar to the contemporary Third World situation. In this sense, Third World Christians, in theory at least, should be in a position to have certain direct and fresh insights into the message of the Bible.

The first theologian who has helped in understanding the role of human history in the construction of a theological expression is Gustavo Gutierrez. His well-known work was first published in 1971 in Spanish and later in 1973 in English under the title "A Theology of Liberation." Right at the beginning of this work, Gutierrez, while re-reading the old well-known Biblical text, says, "In the first place, Charity has been fruitfully rediscovered as the centre of Christian life. This has led to a more Biblical view of the faith as an act of trust, a going out of one's self, a commitment to God and neighbors. Love is the nourishment and the fullness of faith, the gift of one's self to the other, and invariably to others. This is the foundation of the praxis of Christians, of its active presence in history. According to the Bible, faith is the total response of man to God, who saves through love."[9]

The oppressed peoples of Third World countries have been busy constructing for themselves theologies that give meaning to their lives, that affirm their identity and that empower them in their struggle against oppression. Those who have experienced colonial and Christian oppression began to reflect on the meaning of being a church in their own context. This approach resulted in the development of new ways of understanding the meaning of the gospel, the nature of the Church and the missionary mandate, which arose out of the experience of the churches in their local context.

---

[9] M. M. Thomas, *The Acknowledged Christ of the Indian Renaissance* (Madras: CLS, 1970), pp. 314-315.

Some of the liberation theologies, such as Latin American Liberation Theology, Black Theology, Minjung Theology and the Filipino Theology of Struggle, certainly help us in understanding the role of history in the development of Dalit Theology. There is no uniform pattern or easily traceable common features in Third World theological writings. Asia has a wide variety of cultures, experiences and peoples. Yet these writings show certain common concerns and quests derived from common aspects of their socio-cultural and religious background. Their basic common characteristic is that they all attempt to respond to the gospel from their own situations and to give a Third World expression of Christianity.

Latin American Liberation Theology

Latin American Liberation Theology is one of the important theologies that is still operative in our context today. Economic liberation is the basis of this theology. Although its traditional doctrinaire Marxist analysis is inadequate in the context of socio-economic realities of India, its option for the poor and the oppressed is useful. But it needs to be questioned because it neglects the caste factor that adds to the complexity of Indian socio-economic realities. The Liberation Theology that is emerging in the Indian context is not a replica of the Latin American Liberation Theology. It certainly uses Marxian tools of analysis and it may be still effective in our context to some extent. Wesley Ariarajah rightly observes thus:

> Thus the churches in Latin America, reflecting on the meaning of the Gospel in the context of poverty and oppression, developed theological methods that insisted on involvement and committed praxis as the starting point for all theological reflection. This led to a theological tradition that saw the Gospel primarily as 'Good News to the Poor.'[10]

---

[10] Wesley Ariarahagm, *Gospel and Culture: An Ongoing Discussion within the Ecumenical Movement, Gospel and Cultures Pamphlets* (Geneva: WCC, 1994), p. 36.

The emancipatory emphasis of Christian practice is the necessary and legitimate corrective to traditional theology.

Water Buffalo Theology

Kosuke Koama of Japan has contributed to his Koyama's water buffalo theology. "He detests theology written in an academic style wherein authors do their best to discourage people from reading them."[11]

> His hermeneutic is strongly people-centered and contextual. All theologies have to be subordinated to the needs of the people concerned. Throughout his writings a serious concern to root theology in the various cultures, religious and historical contexts is found. If there is one theological center in Koyama's thought, it would be the *theologia crucis* of Luther, on whom he wrote his doctoral dissertation. For him, only 'the crucified mind ... can meaningfully participate in authentic contextualization.'[12]

It is firmly rooted in self-denial, 1 Cor. 2:2; Matt.16:24. Throughout his writings, there is the constant interaction with imperialism, both past and present, idolatry of power and wealth in national and international affairs, problems faced by racial, economic, religious and other minorities, ecology and the like in light of the cross of Christ.[13]

Koyama has always pleaded for a more positive attitude towards other religions against the background of the generally negative view taken earlier by Western Christianity. After all, God has not left himself without a witness, Acts 14:17. "Thus he argues that we should avoid speaking of the superiority of Christianity as opposed to Christ as a religion over other religions."[14]

One is not syncretistic simply because he or she affirms that which is good and true in other religions. Koyama's theology displays a strong sensitivity to the socio-political

---

[11] Kosuke Koyama, "The Crucified Christ Challenges Human Power,' in R. S. Sugirtharaj (ed.) Asian *Faces of Jesus* (New York: Orbis Books, 1993), p. 156.

[12] Kosuke Koyama, *Waterbuffalo Theology* (London: SCM, 1974), p. 24.

[13] Yung, Mangoes or Bananas?, p. 163.

[14] Kosuke Koyama, *No Handle on the Cross* (London: SCM, 1977), p. 89.

context of Asia. But it is positively weak in the evangelistic and pastoral dimensions. He takes inculturation seriously, and his apparent indifference to doctrines and implicit religious pluralism raise serious questions about his faithfulness to apostolic faith.

EATWOT Theology

EATWOT Theology is not purely Christian, as its theological framework includes the Marxian analysis. Sinfulness is there in the structures and in the individuals and the evil that is operative seems to be mysterious. So, there is need to expose the sinfulness.[15] EATWOT Theology was and is interested in developing scientifically a theology that spoke with the voice of the poor and the marginalised in history. The EATWOT methodology has not yet spoken about specific oppression, such as caste, in the Indian context, though it has made peripheral references to it in the past. It is yet to come up with an adequate framework of analysis for this specific form of oppression: caste. The EATWOT analysis begins with the emergence of capitalism, that is, with the last 500 years or so of the history of capitalism.

People in Third World countries suffer in the midst of so many conflicts. East Timor, for example, struggles for its independence and freedom from the oppressive domination of Indonesia. There are also numerous accounts of human rights violations and the heinous crimes and cruel abuses suffered by literally millions of women, men and children of India, Japan, Philippines, Burma and so on. Further still are the on-going overt and covert wars that are raging in the region, in which the lives of many young people are being lost. Yet, in the midst of all these cultural, religious, racial and sexist conflicts, people of the Third World struggle against the life-sucking forces of globalisation.

---

[15] Balasundaram, "Dalit Theology and other Theologies," p. 255.

Theology of Transposition

The Theology of Transposition was developed by the best-known Chinese theologian, Song Choan-seng. There are three key ideas in his writings: Rejection of the concept of salvation-history, transposition theology and critique of Christian mission.

Song's Reinterpretation

At the heart of Song's reinterpretation of Christian Theology is his rejection of the salvation history in the Bible as being normative in theology. He observes:

> The crucial question is obviously this: Is the salvation history intensely exhibited or demonstrated in both the Old and the New Testaments to be looked upon as the absolute norm by which events in secular world history get chosen arbitrarily to be incorporated into God's salvation in Christ, or, is it to be regarded as a pattern or a type of God's salvation manifested in a massively concentrated way in ancient Israel and in the history of the church and therefore to be discovered in varied degrees of intensity and concentration in other nations and peoples also.[16]

Song developed his second major theme, the theological methodology of transposition, which he develops in detail in *The Compassionate God* (1982). Transposition for Song is essentially another word for incarnation. He rebuts theological centrism, "which perceives the history of Israel and of Christianity as the controlling factor in theology, as a roadblock that creates a major problem for transpositional theology."[17]

According to him, God is at work in all cultures, nations and religions. This truth became evident to "Deutero-Isaiah" through the traumatic experience of dispersal and is evident in the teachings of Jesus and Paul. He goes on in the second part of the book to argue that the gospel must be fully

---

[16] Song Choan-seng, "New China and Salvation History – A Methodological Inquiry," *S.E. Asia Journal of Theology*, 15:2 (1974), p. 57.

[17] Song Choan-seng, *The Compassionate God. An Exercise in the Theology of Transposition* (New York: Orbis Books, 1982), p. 16.

incarnated into Asia. After all, Christianity is not "change-proof", nor is it a "one-size religion."[18]

"According to Song, Christian mission today is marred by its Western centrism, and an individualistic gospel which makes converts who then become rootless in their own cultures. It is, therefore, in serious need of reconstruction."[19]

"Song identifies creation and redemption. He argues that if God has been redemptively at work in creation, then the church must not just stand on one side guarding itself against 'what is often carelessly labeled as non-Christian cultures'."[20]

"The theological task of Christian mission consists of identifying God's creative work in and judgement upon all cultures, societies, histories and politics."[21] This implies that mission is political. He rejects any emphasis on mission that focuses on personal conversion into a Christianity distorted, as he perceives it, by western-centred hermeneutics.

Song has, in fact, by beginning with his *a priori* denial of the uniqueness of biblical salvation history, changed the gospel into something different. One of his basic criticisms of Western Christian missions in Asia is their general failure to come to terms with the sociopolitical implications of the gospel in the Asian context.[22]

Song argues that the claim to uniqueness is a Western imposition on the Christian faith. He remarks that the Asian Church completely fails to realise that Jesus Christ is intended to bring about a radical social order through a radical change of individual men and women. "Conversion is not simply a

---

[18] *Ibid.,* p. 181.

[19] Song Choan-seng, *Christian Mission in Reconstruction – An Asian Attempt* (Madras: CLS, 1975), p. 18.

[20] *Ibid.,* p. 28.

[21] *Ibid.*

[22] *Ibid.,* p. 122.

personal affair but a social event contributing to the emergence of a new social order."[23]

According to Song, the Church is an event that happens whenever God's work of redemption takes place. And it is not meant to be identified immediately with a 'permanent social organization brought into existence in and through the act of Christ.'[24]

Third World Liberation theologians believe that the orthodox doctrine of God tends to manipulate God in favour of the capitalistic social structure.

Liberation Theology responds by stressing the incomprehensible mysteriousness of the reality of God. The God of the future is the crucified God who submerges himself in a world of misery. "God is found on the crosses of the oppressed rather than in beauty, power, or wisdom."[25]

> Third-World people's suffering is the extent, the sheer magnitude of the suffering. More Asians are hungry, homeless, unemployed and illiterate than all the rest of the world put together. More men and women are despised, humiliated, cheated; more suffer the tyranny of governments and oppressive elites, and the fear and shame that tyranny brings than in all the rest of the world combined... There may be areas of poverty around the world as bad as Asia... but there is nothing anywhere to match the sweep and unrelieved misery of Asia's suffering.[26]

The liberation theologians in Asia, particularly in the Philippines and India, are correct in calling for identification with the economically poor and the politically oppressed.

Korean Minjung Theology

Modernisation policies in South Korea led to a rapid growth of industrialisation, and a corresponding increase in the gross

---

[23] *Ibid.*

[24] Song, *Christian Mission in Reconstruction*, P. 63.

[25] Aristide, "Liberation Theology" at http://mb-soft.com/believe/txn/liberati.htm

[26] Julio Labayen, "Asian Suffering and the Christian Hope", in T. K. Thomas (ed.), *Testimony Amid Suffering* (Singapore: CCA, 1977), p. 9.

national product. In the process, it resulted in an overall economic deprivation of both rural peasants and urban workers characterised by low wages, long hours and hazardous working conditions, as well as a widening gap between the rich and the poor. Against this dehumanising background, a small group of theologians began to develop the idea of a theology of the *minjung*, as a contextual Korean theology.

Meaning of Minjung Theology

"Etymologically, the word means 'the mass of the people, or mass, or just the people'. Theologically, the minjung is present wherever there is 'socio-cultural alienation, economic exploitation and political suppression."[27]

In Korea, churches emphasised the experience of the people and sought to do theology that places the Minjung, that is, the suffering masses, as the subject of theological reflection. Korean Minjung Theology is one of the theologies of identities. It is the theology by the Minjung, the mass of people, and several lay and professional theologians contributed to the emergence of it.

> In the Bible, they are the foreigners, orphans, widows, the poor and the 'sinners', and in practice today poor farmers, exploited industrialized workers, urban squatters, beggars, etc.'[28] Minjung theology is not of, by or for the minjung people. Rather it is the reflection of theologians who have a guilt complex about themselves not being minjung. It tries to understand the minjung's situation in history, their plight, and how they express themselves in their social biography. Minjung tries to learn from them, and through them to trace the genuine message of the Jesus for 'sinners' behind the pages of the New Testament, in relation to justice, love and freedom. 'It is addressed to Christians and the general public.'[29]

---

[27] David Kwang-Sun Suh, "A Biographic Sketch of an Asian Theological Consultation," in Kim Yong Bock (ed.), *In Minjung Theology. People as the Subjects of History* (Singapore: Common on Theological Concerns, 1981), p. 17.

[28] Young-Hak Hyun, "Minjung Theology and the Religion of Han," East Asia Journal Theology, 3.2 (1985) 354.

[29] *Ibid.*

Biblical Paradigms for Minjung Theology

There are at least three biblical paradigms for the theology of the minjung. The first is the exodus event. The second is crucifixion-resurrection, which is also basically political, as it is clear that Jesus was condemned as a political offender. The third is Jesus' mission directed primarily at the *am ha'aretz*, those called 'sinners' — the poor, sick, crippled, tax-collectors, widows and prostitutes — by the religious leaders of the time.

According to David Kwang-Sun Suh, the political movement initiated by Jesus was depoliticised when the Hellenistic church shifted from historical and eschatological thinking to metaphysical thinking and transformed the Messiah of the afflicted minjung into a non-political heavenly Christ. "Later the underground religion of the oppressed ended up as the state religion of the oppressor. But the Church preserved the political and revolutionary nature of Jesus' true teachings in the concept of the Millennium, which symbolizes the historical, earthly, and semi-ultimate aspiration of the minjung."[30]

This concept must be revived as a counter-balance to the concept of the Kingdom of God to prevent Christianity from being reduced to a merely otherworldly faith.

Through the study of the socio-economic history, literature and art forms and religious belief of the minjung, various minjung movements can be uncovered. Included among these are the Donghak revolution of the late nineteenth century against both feudal and foreign oppressions and the 1960 Student Revolution inspired by democratic concerns. "These three paradigms from the Bible, church history, and minjung history form the bases for the emerging theology."[31]

---

[30] Suh, "Historical References for a Theology of Minjung", p. 162.

[31] Yung, *Mangoes or Bananas?* p. 180.

Methodological Tools

Minjung Theology claims to be a reinterpretation of the mission Dei for Korea today. With respect to the contextual and missiological theology, that of socio-political relevance, there is no doubt at all that minjung theologians are firmly on target. The indifference of the vast majority of the Korean churches to political repression and economic exploitation from the 1960s onwards is well summed up by Kim Se-yoon: "While some liberal Christians have fought courageously against the oppressive regimes on behalf of the poor and oppressed, the vast majority of Korean Christians have remained politically neutral or silent."[32] Minjung theology's concern for socio-political transformation poses a fundamental challenge to Korean Christianity today.

Limitations of Minjung Theology

"One of the best premises of its biblical hermeneutics is that Jesus' original gospel of political liberation was transformed by the Early Church into a message of religious salvation."[33]

It was further asserted that this was further abetted by the missionaries who came to Korea. Even as Koreans increasingly looked to the Christian message for national and socio-political salvation, the missionaries sought to depoliticise and denationalise it by spiritualising it.[34] In Minjung Theology, salvation is primarily political. The spiritual dimension hardly features.

Minjung Theology is both positive and negative towards inculturation. Positively, it seeks to employ the methods that are indigenous to Korea. It also takes inculturation seriously in its deliberate efforts to transcend the dualism

---

[32] Kim Se-yoon, "Is "Minjung Theology" a Christian Theology?" Calvin Theology Journal. 22:2 (1987), p. 259.

[33] Suh, "Historical References for a Theology of Minjung", p. 162.

[34] Suh, "A Biographic Sketch of an Asian Theological Consultation", pp. 21-26.

inherent in much of Western theology, particularly in its reinterpretation of Korean church history.[35]

It actually looks more like a theology, strongly shaped by various liberal versions of Western political, liberation and secular theologies, and merely given a Korean dress.

Seo Nam Dong's Minjung Theology

Theological reflections were started by Seo Nam Dong in the 1970s, and Minjung Theology was also influenced by context. Especially theologians who directly implanted western theology into theological schools and churches without reflections felt shame and repented of their sycophancy. Their theological perspective start from Minjung's sufferings and they try to be with Minjung's life. Therefore, theologians called their theology as "Minjung Theology." During the time of political upheaval, Minjung Theology was the sign and direction of the democrative radical Christian movement and anti-American imperial movement in South Korea.

Theology of the Oppressed

During the past two decades, liberation theologians in Latin America have demonstrated a remarkable capacity to interpret and illuminate the liberation struggles of the poor and oppressed people in their respective countries. They try to provide the poor and the oppressed with a new understanding of God, sin, salvation and Jesus Christ. "The theology of liberation can succinctly be worked out through three profiles: an incarnational logic, an eschatological horizon and the 'poor' as hermeneutic tool for praxis."[36]

---

[35] Chai-Yong Choo, "A Brief Sketch of Korean Christian History from Minjung Perspective, in Kim Yong Bock (ed.), *In Minjung Theology. People as the Subjects of History* (Singapore: Common on Theological Concerns, 1981), p. 69.

[36] Antony Kalliath "Revisiting Liberation Theology in a Neo-Liberal World I," *Vidyajyoti Journal of Theological Reflection*, Vol. 72, No. 3, March 2008, 169.

Theology of the Sufferings

The struggle for the cultural, ethical and religious values that defend the lives of the oppressed is not an abstract or ideological struggle, however, but a real-life experience that takes place within the popular movements in the Third World. This struggle is an essential part of the struggle for life and an integral part of the historic struggle for liberation from oppression.

In the last ten years, theology has expanded its concept of "the poor" and "the oppressed" to refer not only to economic condition, but also to race, culture and gender. The poor and the oppressed are not only those who are economically poor, but also people of indigenous or African descent; and women, especially Third World women, who are doubly exploited—as poor people and as women.[37]

There is a greater space for theology of the oppressed to develop within popular movements than is possible within armed struggles. Likewise, it finds a privileged site for creativity and development in the cultural, ethical and religious struggles of the people. The current international context offers theology of the oppressed a greater potential for growth and maturation and a challenge to consciously and critically respond to the urgent needs of the oppressed people.

The struggle for liberation involves not only the interpretation of reality, but also a commitment to its transformation. We are challenged to create a new society where no one is poor, oppressed or excluded, and everyone has life and dignity. Liberation Theology does not reflect on an abstract or universal faith, but rather on a faith that is lived in the midst of struggling to transform society.[38]

---

[37] Pablo Richard, "Liberation Theology in the New International Context— New Themes and Challenges" in http://mb-soft.com/believe/txn/liberati.htm

[38] *Ibid.*

While traditional theology used Western philosophy as a basis for reflection, Liberation Theology uses the critical and liberating perspectives of the social sciences—including elements of Marxism—to identify the root causes of oppression and to reflect critically on acting to overcome this oppression in society. Liberation Theology has never attempted to set forth a new theology, but rather a new way of doing theology—from the perspective of the poor and their struggle for justice and liberation.[39]

Liberation Theology

Liberation Theology was born out of the participation of the Christians in the liberation struggles of Latin America in the 1960s and 1970s. It matured as the Church began to reflect critically on their faith and their actions on behalf of social justice. The theme of Liberation Theology has always been the revelation of God to the poor as a lived experience, which is celebrated in community and reflected on within the context of the liberation process.[40]

Gustavo Gutierrez, a Peruvian Roman Catholic priest, the one who first used the term "Liberation Theology", defines theology as "critical reflection on historical praxis." Doing theology requires the theologian to be immersed in his or her own intellectual and socio-political history. Theology is not a system of timeless truths, engaging the theologian in the repetitious process of systematisation and apologetic argumentation. Theology is a dynamic, ongoing exercise involving contemporary insights into knowledge (epistemology), man (anthropology) and history (social analysis). "Praxis" means more than the application of theological truth to a given situation. It means the discovery and the formation of theological truth out of a given historical

---

[39] *Ibid.*

[40] *Ibid.*

situation through personal participation in the Latin American class struggle for a new socialist society.[41]

The profound changes in the lives of the poor in the Third World radically challenge Liberation Theology in every way: its vision of the world, its commitment to liberation, its pastoral practice and its ethics and spirituality. The preferential option for the poor requires us to commit ourselves to defend the lives of this condemned and excluded majority in the Third World, which is currently experiencing an accelerated process of deterioration and disintegration.[42]

Significant hermeneutical and exegetical developments are emerging in relation to the Bible and the existential reality in constructing a Christological and theological expression and context of Jesus Christ's identification with the oppressed, the marginalised and the exploited. This movement has proved to be not only instrumental, but also inspirational for those suffering people who have wanted to derive a greater significance and identification in their Christian faith, theological expression and missiological witness. It became necessary to unravel the Christian faith, expression and understanding from Western philosophy, ideology and syncretism, enabling the oppressed peoples to liberate the Word of God from the oppressive indoctrination of the West, to incorporate the Christian stories into their context and culture, endeavouring a radical change in hermeneutical and exegetical scholarship.

Richard observes that Liberation Theology is developed because of the option for the poor and commitment to keep alive the hope of the poor for life. But Liberation Theology will survive only if theologians analyse the current

---

[41] Gustavo Gutierrez, "A Theology of Liberation" quoted by Jean-Bertrand Aristide, "Liberation Theology." at http://mb-soft.com/believe/txn/liberati.htm

[42] Richard, "Liberation Theology in the New International Context—New Themes and Challenges." http://mb-soft.com/believe/txn/liberati.htm

international context and develop a theology that is faithful both to the original spirit and methodology of Liberation Theology and to the challenges of the future. There is a need to develop a theology that resists death and affirms life and, at the same time, renews faith in a God of the poor and a God of life.[43]

Liberation Theology has the potential to offer hope to the poor and the oppressed of the world. Its future, however, is inseparable from the future of all peoples on earth whose lives are threatened — and of the very earth itself. Ultimately, what is at stake is the life of the poor on earth.

Theology of the oppressed is more a movement that attempts to unite theology and socio-political concerns than a new school of theological theory. It is more accurate to speak of Liberation Theology in the plural, for these theologies of liberation find contemporary expression among the Blacks, feminists, Asians, Hispanic Americans and Native Americans. The most significant and articulate expression to date has taken place in Latin America. Theological themes have been developed in the Latin American context, which have served as models for other theologies of liberation.[44]

There are at least four major factors that have played a significant role in the formulation of Latin American Liberation Theology. First, it is a post-Enlightenment theological movement. Leading proponents such as Gustavo Gutierrez, Juan Segundo and Jose Miranda are responsive to the epistemological and social perspectives of Kant, Hegel and Marx. Second, Liberation Theology has been greatly influenced by European political theology, finding in J. B. Metz, Jurgen Moltmann and Harvey Cox perspectives that have criticised the historical and individualistic nature of existential theology. Third, it is for the most part a Roman

---

[43] *Ibid.*

[44] Jean-Bertrand Aristide, "Liberation Theology." in http://mb-soft.com/believe/txn/liberati.htm

Catholic theological movement. Liberation Theology has been identified with the Roman Catholic Church. A significant number of Latin American leaders within the Roman Catholic Church turned to Liberation Theology as the theological voice for the Latin American Church. Fourth, it is a theological movement specifically and uniquely situated in the Latin American context. Liberation theologians contend that their continent has been victimised by colonialism, imperialism and multinational corporations. Economic "developmentalism" has placed the so-called underdeveloped Third World nations in a situation of dependence, resulting in the local economies of Latin America being controlled by decisions made in New York, Houston, or London. In order to perpetuate this economic exploitation, liberationists argue, the powerful capitalist countries give military and economic support to secure certain political regimes supportive of the economic status quo. These four factors combine to bring about a distinctive theological method and interpretation.[45]

Liberation Theology accepts the two-pronged "challenge of the Enlightenment." These two critical elements shape Liberation Theology's biblical hermeneutic. The first challenge comes through the philosophical perspective begun by Immanuel Kant, which argued for the autonomy of human reason. Theology is no longer worked out in response to God's self-disclosure through the divine-human authorship of the Bible. This revelation from "outside" is replaced by the revelation of God found in the matrix of human interaction with history. The second challenge comes through the political perspective founded by Karl Marx, which argues that man's wholeness can be realised only through overcoming the alienating political and economic structures of society. The role of Marxism in Liberation Theology must be honestly understood.[46]

---

[45] *Ibid.*

[46] Juan Sobrino, quoted by Jean-Bertrand Aristide, "Liberation Theology" in http://mb-soft.com/ believe/txn/liberati.htm

The challenge of the Enlightenment is followed by the challenge of the Latin American situation in formulating Liberation Theology's hermeneutics of praxis. The important hermeneutical key emerging out of the Latin American context is summarised in Hugo Assmann's reference to the "epistemological privilege of the poor." On a continent where the majority is both poor and Roman Catholic, Liberation Theology claims the struggle is with man's inhumanity to man and not with unbelief.[47]

Liberation theologians have carved out a special place for the poor. All communion with God is predicated on opting for the poor and exploited classes, identifying with their plight and sharing their fate. Jesus secularises the means of salvation, making the sacrament of the "other" a determining element for entry into the Kingdom of God. The poor are the epiphany of the Kingdom or of the infinite exteriority of God.[48]

People who are saying "No" to anti-life forces and "Yes" to human freedom and dignity have made common cause with people who affirm that as subjects of history they are committed to a radical process that will ensure their true liberation and authentic humanhood. In such a process, they have demonstrated a spirituality not only of meditation, but also a spirituality of involvement and engagement of active obedience, and collective commitment towards a new social order and political well-being; of sacrifice and service to the people that is embodied in a life-style of economic discipline, sharing and mutuality; of a sense of enmity and anger to those things that cause the sufferings of many; of undying courage and love and of longings for justice and freedom for all.[49] Such a spirituality means no less than an act of

---

[47] Aristide, "Liberation Theology" in http://mb-soft.com/believe/txn/liberati.htm

[48] *Ibid.*

[49] Feliciano Carino, "What About the Theology of Struggle?" in *Religion and Society*, Manila: FIDES, 1988, p. xii.

sharing in the broken Body of Christ for the healing of the world, a commitment to the mandate to give oneself to God and to the world so that God may be honoured and that all may enjoy God's gracious gift of fullness of life.

Liberation Theology holds that in the death of the peasant or the native Indian, we are confronted with "the monstrous power of the negative. We are forced to understand God from within history mediated through the lives of oppressed human beings. God is not recognised analogically in creation's beauty and power, but dialectically in the creature's suffering and despair." Sorrow "triggers the process of cognition," enabling us to comprehend God and the meaning of his will. Combining post-Enlightenment critical reflection with an acute awareness of Latin America's conflict-ridden history results in several important theological perspectives.[50]

Liberation Theology holds that through Jesus' life people are brought to the liberating conviction that God does not remain outside history, indifferent to the present course of evil events but that he reveals himself through the authentic medium of the poor and the oppressed.[51]

The strength of the theology of the oppressed is in its compassion for the poor and its conviction that the Christian should not remain passive and indifferent to their plight. Man's inhumanity to man is sin and deserves the judgment of God and Christian resistance. This theology is a plea for costly discipleship and a reminder that follows Jesus has practical social and political consequences. The theology of the oppressed rightly exposes the fact of oppression in society and the fact that there are the oppressor and the oppressed. The Christian understands sin and alienation from God as a dilemma confronting both the oppressor and the oppressed.

---

[50] Aristide, "Liberation Theology" in http://mb-soft.com/believe/txn/liberati.htm

[51] *Ibid.*

Indian Christian Theology for Constructing Dalit Theology

The Indian Christian Theology is a rich mix like India. It is old, and ancient tradition has it that there has existed a church in South India from the time of the apostles. But at the same time, it is new because it continues to address fresh and exciting challenges, as evidenced by the theologies produced by Indian Christian Dalits, the Adivasis and oppressed Indian Christian women. Its theological thinking reflects denominational perceptions ranging from those of churches of the orthodox tradition to the theological formulations of newly formed protestant ecumenical institutions such as the Church of South India and the Church of North India. It is confessional, but takes the pluralistic religious context seriously for its theological articulation. It is spiritual but not blind to the socio-economic reality of the present, which is oppressive and divisive.

> In Indian Christian theology, there have been two dominant expressions of theology in use. The first one came with Western missionaries and with the passage of time, it became the major area of study under the name 'systematic theology' in our country. The second one is the traditional 'Indian Christian Theology', which basically came into existence with the efforts made by some of the so-called upper-caste converts as their response to their faith. 'Both these expressions centered around the study of God, having in their mind the Greek connotation of the expressions 'theology', as the science of Pure Being or God.[52]

Indian Christian theologians have accepted three main sources for Indian Christian theology, based upon Indian classical Hinduism, what they named as *pramanas* or authority. The first one is Sruti or the inspired Scriptures, the second one is *anubhava* or personal experiences of God and the third one is *anumana* or inference or reason. Most of the earlier Indian Christian theologians continued to operate within the ongoing traditions of Hinduism.

---

[52] Williams, N. P., "What Is Theology?" in Kenneth E. Erik (ed.) *The Study of Theology* (London, n.p. 1939), p.3.

As James Massey rightly points out, "The roots of Indian Christian Theology lie in the experiences of mostly upper caste/class Christian converts of this century and the last century,"[53] it was searching for an indigenous expression of Christianity, which forms an important element in Indian Christian Theology.

Most of the contents the Indian Christian Theology did not address itself to reflect the issues that the majority of the Christians faced either before or after they became Christians. Its concern has not been to search for an Indian expression of their new faith. What the poor Christians of the Indian Church are searching for even today is how to earn their daily bread and how to overcome their life situation of oppression, poverty, suffering, injustice, illiteracy and denial of identity.

Indian Christian Theology, thus, cannot but be intrinsically intertwined with human life and how this can be lived collectively before God. The famous Indian evangelist-scholar, Sadhu Sundar Singh, spoke of his desire to be able to give to his fellow countrymen "the water of life in an Indian cup." The gospel came to people in a particularised and concrete form and not as an abstract universal principle. It has resulted in the formulations of what is now known as Indian Christian Theology.

The missing part in Indian Christian Theology is the experience of Christian Dalits. The roots of the current Indian Christian Theology lie in the experiences of mostly upper-caste Christian converts of this century and the last century. Another expression of Indian Christian Theology needs to be worked out, which would be relevant to the living situation of the vast majority of the Dalits as well.

---

[53] James Massey, "Ingredients for a Dalit Theology", in R. S. Sugirtharajah & Cecil Hargreaves (eds.), *Readings in Indian Christian Theology* (Delhi: ISPCK, 1995), p. 152.

"Certain features of this Brahminic culture were adapted in Christian practice and was projected as Indian and forced on the Indian church, a predominantly Dalit Church."[54]

The attempt was to reformulate biblical theology in Indian categories of thought, in a manner relevant to the Indian context. Until recently, Western theology has dominated the Indian theological scene, and Christianity has come under criticism from Hindu thinkers in this regard.

> The pioneers of Indian theology were not Christians but enlightened Hindus who came under the strong influence of Western thought and Christianity. These enlightened nationalists wanted to reform Hinduism and Indian society, thereby counterbalancing Christian missionary activities. For Indian Christian leaders, Indian theology is an attempt to meet the criticism that Christianity is a foreign and dangerous denationalizing force. It represents a search for and an expression of self-identity in India and in the field of Christian theology. It is an attempt to conceptualize the urge for being Christian and Indian simultaneously. It faces the challenge of renascent Hinduism in its relegation of Christianity to a subordinate status. Moreover, it stands for the concern of Indian theologians to communicate the gospel in thought patterns familiar to the Indian mind. It is to present 'the water of life in an Indian cup.'[55]

"Indian Christian theological reflections generally accept the dominant versions and interpretation of Hindu religious myths without questioning whose purpose and identity they serve."[56] Much of the existing Indian Christian theology tries to relate to the dominant stream.

The roots of Indian Christian Theology lie in the experiences of mostly upper-class/caste Christian converts of this century and the last century. In fact, Indian Christian Theology is very much attached to the Brahminical culture and ideology. For many of the Indian Christian theologians,

---

[54] Devasahayam, "Doing Dalit Theology: Basic Assumptions," p. 272.

[55] C V Mathew, "Contextual Theology", http://www.nathaniel.turner.com/contextualtheology.htm

[56] A. M. Abraham Ayoorkuzhiel, "Dalit Theology: A Movement of Counter-Culture," in James Massey (ed.), *Indigenous People: Dalits – Dalit Issues in Today's Theological Debate* (Delhi: ISPCK, 1994), p. 260.

cultural contextuality meant adjustment to the dominant ethos and even to such structures as caste.

"The *vedas, upanishads*, and their renowned commentators exercised a great deal of influence on these theologians. These thinkers and their experiences were very much different from the majority of Christians, who were poor and belonged to the lower strata of the society."[57]

Aravind P. Nirmal, one of the pioneers in Christian Dalit Theology, had made the same kind of observation in one of his articles in the early 1970s: Indian Christian Theology has perpetuated within itself what I prefer to call the "Brahminic" tradition. This tradition has further perpetuated intuition — an inferiority-oriented approach to the theological task in India. The Third World theology with its allegiance to Liberation Theology seemed relevant to the situation of India, where a majority of the Indian people face the problem of poverty.

Indian Christian Theology, whether it is the traditional one or the recent Third World Theology, has failed to see suffering and the ongoing struggle of Indian Dalits for liberation as subject matter appropriate for doing theology in India.

> What is surprising here is the reality that fifty to eighty percent of Christians are of Dalits in origin. That means the Christian population numbering over 25 millions, about 20 millions, are from the Dalit background. In other words, the Indian theologians have virtually ignored the social reality of Indian Church. To put it in another way, the concern for subaltern identity, which should have been the major area of theological reflection, was not at all pursued in Indian Theological thinking.[58]

Aravind P. Nirmal, who himself is a Dalit, believes that the authentic Dalit Theology will be based on their own Dalit experiences, their own sufferings, their own aspirations and

---

[57] Kuruvila "Dalit Theology: An Indian Christian Attempt to Give Voice to the Voiceless."

[58] *Ibid.*

their own hopes. It will be the story of their pathos and their protest against the socio- economic injustices they have been subjugated to throughout history. The shortcoming in Indian Christian Theology paves the way for the development of Dalit Theology. It has been pointed out that:

> The insensitivity of the Church and Indian Christian theology to Dalit concerns and the deeper dimension of their struggle and aspirations for fuller humanity, despite the majority of Christians being of Dalit origin, makes imperative the formulation of a Christian Dalit theology, with a universal appeal.[59]

It has, to an extent, made the gospel relevant in the context of Indian nationalism, religio-cultural pluralism and socio-economic development. It marks the beginning of Indian biblical scholarship and creative theological formulations. Yet none has managed to be faithful to Christian Theology in its entirety, nor to the context and content simultaneously. Quite often, the "context" has become more decisive than the "text", and this is critical.[60]

Abraham Ayrookuzhiel talks of Dalit Theology as counter culture in relation to the brahmanical culture that continues to serve the interests of the privileged sections in society. He believes that Dalit Theology is a spiritual movement for meaning in life, self-fulfilment and freedom.

The early Indian Church had been challenged with a call to harmony of all religions. The Indian Church could not simply depend on the theological apologetics of the past. Fresh answers were given from within the Indian context. Many Indian Christian theologies have attempted to reformulate Christian Theology in a manner relevant to the Indian context. These attempts have provided different models, depending on the particular framework and the concerns of the gospel expressed through the framework. Though there is no single pattern or model for the

---

[59] Prabhakar, "The Search for a Dalit Theology," p. 203.

[60] Mathew, "Contextual Theology", http://www.nathaniel.turner.com/contextualtheology.htm

development of Indian Christian Theology, the key to Indian Theology is the discernment of the reality of Christ and His mission on frontiers of the Church both with other faiths and with the struggle for justice.

Summary

Many interesting theological developments have taken place throughout the world amongst the oppressed, the outcastes, the suffering poor and the marginalised. Most of these types of theology failed to find in the struggles of Indian Dalits subject matter appropriate for doing theology in India. A substantial part of the Christian population in India consists of people from the Scheduled Castes and Scheduled Tribes background. This fact should have provided an authentic liberation motif for Indian Christian Theology. If our theologians failed to see this in the past, it is all the more reason why we need to wake up to this reality today and seriously apply ourselves to the task of doing Dalit Theology. This can be done by responding positively to the reality and struggle of the Dalits in India.

The brutal reality of poverty and oppression experienced by the majority of humankind in many parts of the Third World paved the way for the theology of the oppressed. The living and social conditions in the Third World gave birth to Liberation Theology. As long as poverty and oppression exist and as long as there are Christians who critically reflect on their faith in the context of the struggle for justice and life, Liberation Theology will continue to exist and develop further.

Chapter 4

Constructing Dalit Theology

Liberation is very much needed for the suffering and downtrodden people of India. Those who are suffering because of caste hierarchy should be relieved from their pathos. For the liberation of the Dalits, we need to foster Dalit Theology based on a new ideology.

Process of Constructing Dalit Theology

The term "theology" comes from the Greek terms, *theos* and *logos*. It means word of God or word about God. The concept of God is the chief concern of theology. It is God who is the ultimate authority and point of reference for the theologian. The concepts related to Scripture, creed and humanity are secondary and derivative from the concept of God.

Recently, there have been a number of new voices offering a counter-theology to the existing and dominant Sanskritically-based theology. The most vociferous and vibrant are the Dalits, the Adivasis and Indian women. These groups have their own distinctive experiences and different histories and represent dissimilar socio-economic and political categories. But what is common to all of them is that they have been marginalised and alienated by the ideological and theological conceptions of the prevailing Indian Christian theologies. Dalit Theology is the expression of the commitment of Dalit theologians to the Dalits.

Content for Constructing Dalit Theology

Dalit Theology has to discern more clearly the fact of God working in human history, particularly the Dalit history, seeing God as the saviour of Indian history through the Dalits and subaltern communities. Dalit Theology recognises the indispensability of social analysis in theologising, analysing society from a caste perspective; it is built on the historical consciousness of the Dalits and seeks to sensitise and further intensify this consciousness.

Firstly, it is a theology related to the Dalits or theological reflection on the Christian responsibility to the depressed classes. Secondly, it is a theology for the depressed classes or the message addressed to the Dalits to which they seem to be responding. Thirdly, it is a theology from the depressed classes, that is, the theology they would like to expound. "Theology is the ordering of a system of ideas based upon beliefs about the revelation of God."[1]

Constructing Dalit Theology by Experience

Theology needs to deal with the ultimate and the impending issues of life and death, especially about those who have been despised are degraded. So, a theology of Dalits and for the Dalits should entail Dalit experience and reflection. "Theology is foundational to Christian faith and practice; just as worldview of a certain cultural tradition is foundational to group members' belief and practice."[2]

Dalit Theology is a reflection on Dalit human experience from the perspective of Dalit faith. Dalit life is the focus of Dalit Theology. Dalit Theology is not mainly concerned with religious metaphysic or rituals, not even with soul after death, but with human person as he or she lives in the world of theology. Dalit Theology must reflect on contemporary forms of human experiences and life—all of which must be related to, relativised and humanised by the concept of God.

Dalit Theology Is a Doing Theology

> Dalit theology is also a doing theology because it puts into practice the theological objectives to challenge and eradicate the cruel injustices, harsh treatment and prolonged oppressiveness faced by

---

[1] Cone, "The Social Context of Theology," p. 24.

[2] Wan, "Critiquing the Method of Traditional Western Theology and Calling for Sino-Theology."

the Dalit masses. It is also conscientizing the Dalits in the context of their sufferings and struggles for building a new life-order. It further creates awareness among them that their position in life is not simply to undergo sufferings as their destiny but to take responsibility and to involve themselves in social change in order to remove their miserable, degraded and lowly existence.[3]

In their struggle against the historical and contemporary process of domination, the Dalits became conscious of their identity as people in society.

Inspiration drawn from the struggles of the blacks and black theology movement in the United States of America and the people's theology in Korea have been mainly instrumental for pioneering a Dalit theology in India. Although the Christian Dalits form only a small portion of the Dalit community as a whole, the task of theologizing by them will provide for them in their struggle the motivating force to liberate themselves in solidarity with all other Dalits across their religious and sub-caste loyalties.[4]

To be in solidarity with our fellow Dalits belonging to different faiths and ideologies is a demand that God of the Bible, through his own act of incarnation, is putting on us as Christian Dalits.

This is an important factor for the authenticity of Dalit theology, which ultimately will become an instrument of destroying social and religious structures, which are responsible for the on-going historical captivity of the Dalits.[5]

The emerging and experimental nature of Dalit Theology seems to suggest a degree of innovation and a willingness on the part of theologians to explore new ideas.

Dalit theology is an emerging theology and it is in the process of development. Nevertheless, it has occupied world-wide recognition and is used by people from all walks of life. It is regarded as the most significant event in the theological endeavour. Being an indigenous theology, it is more contextual and human-hood praxis oriented.[6]

---

[3] Aruldoss, *Why Dalit Theology?* pp. 29-30.

[4] Kuruvila "Dalit Theology: An Indian Christian Attempt to Give Voice to the Voiceless."

[5] James Massey, *Roots of Dalit History, Christianity, Theology and Spirituality* (Delhi: ISPCK, 1996), p. 87.

[6] Aruldoss, *Why Dalit Theology?*, p. 1.

> Dalit theology is quite different and distinct from dominant
> theologies. Its entry, content, approach, constituency and
> methodology vary. It is apparent that it challenges the universally
> valid norm, acceptable framework and agreed method that conforms
> to western rationality and epistemology.[7]

Dalit Theology is also theo-centric because it expresses the saving action and liberating presence of God. It undergirds God as well as Jesus Christ as the launching pad in its theological process "It reveals the liberating power of God in Jesus Christ who responded to the cry of the poor, the dehumanized and the alienated."[8]

Though the Dalit theological movement is an attempt towards an Indian liberation theology based on the culture and history of the Dalits, it is dependent on the ideological movements originally initiated by periyar E. V. Ramaswamy Naicker, B. R. Ambedkar and Dalit Panthers of Maharastra, who in turn, were influenced by Marxism and the Black movements. It is a theology based on certain borrowed ideologies articulated exclusively for these classes but not by the depressed-class Christians themselves or rooted in their historical experiences; the issue is not authenticity but history.

> The final goal of Dalit theology is to create the possibility of full
> liberation to Dalits. Basing upon the Christ-event of redemption,
> which will involve freeing the Dalits from the oppressive structures,
> make it possible to become subject of human or their own history
> or even have an experience of personal sins' forgiveness, and also
> to achieve the salvation for all the people of God including their
> oppressors. Thus Dalit theology will enable Dalits to become an
> instrument for establishing a just society.[9]

Contextualising Dalit Theology

For constructing a Christian Dalit Theology, it cannot be simply the gaining of the rights, the reservations and

---

[7] John Mohan Razu, "Contours and Trajectories of Dalit Theology", in Samson Prabahakar and Jinkwan Kwon (eds.) *Dalit and Minjung Theologies-A Dialogue* (Bangalore: BTESSC/SATHRI, 2006), p. 48.

[8] Aruldoss, *Why Dalit Theology?* pp. 28-29.

[9] James Massey, "A Review of Dalit Theology", in Samson Prabahakar and Jinkwan Kwon (eds.) *Dalit and Minjung Theologies - A Dialogue* (Bangalore: BTESSC/SATHRI, 2006), p. 9.

privileges. The goal is the realisation of our full humanness or conversely, our full divinity, the ideal of the *imago Dei*, the image of God in us. "To use another biblical metaphor, our goal is the glorious liberty of the children of God."[10]

Dalit Theology is both inclusive and exclusive. Although it is in favour of a specific community, it includes other religious traditions and movements that are engaged in the struggle for justice.

> Dalit theology is another expression of Indian Christian theology based on the living experiences of Dalit themselves, which have been neglected in the earlier Indian Christian Theology. It comes as a powerful voice from the Dalit people in their language and for the service of the people. As a constructing theology it seeks to confront situations of oppression perpetuated by the dominant religious traditions without neglecting the ecumenical concern for one human community. As a matter of fact, an active commitment to peace and justice becomes an integral concern of this theological enterprise. It can also provide an opportunity for the non-Dalits a repentance of their past participation either directly or indirectly in the unjust structures, practices and attitudes produced and nurtured by the caste system.[11]

Background for Constructing Dalit Theology

The modern Dalit movement began with what Christian missionaries now call the people movements. These were localised, grass roots, somewhat simultaneous, conversion movements initiated and led by the Dalits. Dalit Theology can also be called Liberative Theology. It can be even regarded as Indian Liberation Theology, because it is neither an academic discipline nor an intellectual activity with little or no direct contact with the realities. "On the contrary, it activates the suffering masses to pursue and to accomplish their liberation. In other words, it provides a policy for vigorous action to attain their liberation."[12]

---

[10] Arvind Nirmal, "Towards a Christian Theology" in M. E. Prabhakar (ed.), *Towards a Dalit Theology* (Delhi: ISPCK, 1988), p. 133.

[11] Kuruvila "Dalit Theology: An Indian Christian Attempt to Give Voice to the Voiceless."

[12] Aruldoss, *Why Dalit Theology?* p. 30.

The liberation the Dalits experienced in Christ embraced their Dalitness instead of rejecting it as something to be completely left behind. "Dalit Christian" thus seems to be the more accurate label at this stage of their history.

"Dalit theology is firmly grounded on transformation, liberation and change. It is not divorced from politics and ethics. However, the Gospel that undergirds these values emulates the truth of 'life in all its fullness'." [13]

Dalit Theology seeks to work out a theology of liberation for the Dalits in the Indian context. It is different from Liberation Theology to some extent. Liberation Theology reckons all the poor, irrespective of caste, colour and creed. But Dalit Theology is particular about one specific community, that is, the Dalits, and its main and primary concern is their liberation from the clutches of all oppressive systems. Dalit Theology cannot be viewed only from the economic standpoint. "The caste system and the institution of untouchability should also be investigated, since it becomes the primary cause for their poverty."[14]

The current Indian Christian Theology is not really relevant to the living situations of the majority of Indian Christians, who come form the lower strata of society. The missing part in it is the experience of the lowliest of people.[15]

Similar to liberation theologians, Dalit theologians claim methodological exclusivism for Dalit theology and assert that the articulation of Dalit theology is a new way of doing theology.

Dalit Christian Theology is required to take the world of the Dalits seriously. Their awareness of God and their knowledge about the liberating God did not leave them to be aloof and subjugators of oppressive powers. They created

---

[13] Razu, "Contours and Trajectories of Dalit Theology", p. 50.

[14] Aruldoss, *Why Dalit Theology?* p.16.

[15] Massey, "Ingredients for a Dalit Theology", p. 58.

their theology in order to achieve their freedom and liberation. However, "it is recognized in the framework of a universal theology."[16]

Another reason for its emergence is the failure of Indian Christian Theology. When theology is formed, the context ought to be related for transformation of the situations. But Indian Christian Theology has failed to heed the life situation of the Dalits. It failed to take into account the sufferings, aspirations and hopes of the Dalits, who are the main body of the Indian Church. The age-old cry of the Dalits was not at all regarded by Indian Christian Theology, which is very much concerned about the doctrines rather than the horizontal relation. The failure to identify the reality of the Dalits was the basic reason for the emergence of Dalit Theology. Even the missionaries were concentrating on the theology of saving souls rather than social reforms.

Arvind Nirmal states that in our search for Dalit Theology it is well worth remembering that what we are looking for is community-identity, community-roots and community consciousness. The vision of Dalit Theology ought to be unitive vision or a communitive vision.[17] The non-recognition of Dalit Christians in the Indian Church made them seek for an alternative and Dalit Theology eventually became the outcome to fulfill their aspirations.

Biblical Paradigms Constructing Dalit Theology

Biblical paradigms have created awareness among the enlightened Dalit Christians. They have begun to understand the God of the Bible as an initiator and upholder of the human struggles for liberation. The Bible also gave them a theological basis in their struggle for liberation.

The exodus became the most prominent event in the process of Dalit Theology. Dalit Christians realised God as

---

[16] Aruldoss, *Why Dalit Theology?* pp.15-16.

[17] Nirmal, "Towards a Christian Theology," p. 130.

the one who identifies himself with the oppressed and extends his solidarity to liberate them from the system of slavery. Although exodus happened at a particular period and in a particular place, the Dalits did not consider it as a past event but took it as a structuring principle that determines the way of their liberation.

Exodus attracted the Dalits because it occurred when the Israelites were at the apex of slavery. Like the Dalits in India, the Israelites were in an inescapable situation. The Dalits, therefore, took the exodus as an inspiring and stimulating event that led them towards their freedom.

The exodus also helped the Dalits to comprehend that God could not remain indifferent to victimisation and his justice could not remain neutral when injustice become apparent. They also understood that God would act more violently when the oppression is more influential. In other words, when the oppression is carried to the extreme, the liberating act of God becomes necessarily violent. "For God is biased towards the oppressed and punishes the oppressors. He did not respect the lives of the oppressors because oppression is never justifiable in his eyes."[18]

> The Dalits who are living in bondage and slavery find inspirations as well as an answer for their deliverance in the biblical paradigms like the exodus. The exodus event also boosted courage and confidence in the minds of the Dalits, which ultimately pushed them to be the creators of Dalit Theology.[19]

Dalit Theology is an indigenous theology since it has emerged out of the Indian context and out of the self-generated and self-directed Dalit consciousness. It is built on the historical heritage and living experiences of the Dalits.

> The staunch faith in God as the liberator and the community consciousness geared the Dalits to make the Dalit possible. It is also the theological expression of the Dalits in their struggle for social change in order to have meaningful life in society. It aims to provide

---

[18] Aruldoss, *Why Dalit Theology?*, p. 22.

[19] *Ibid.*, p. 23.

useful strategies to achieve their goal that is liberty, equality and fraternity.[20]

Dalit theology is an alternative form of theological endeavour. It arose as a counter-theology when the philosophical-theological approach of the Indian Christian Theology became futile and ineffectual to fulfill the aspirations of the Dalits.[21]

K. C. Abraham, President of Ecumenical Association for the Third World Theologians, rightly points out: "Dalit Theology emerges out of the attempt in their seeking a new identity for themselves based on their past religions and cultures which had been suppressed or destroyed by dominant communities.[22]

Dalit Theology is also a counter-theology. "It questions as well as criticizes the Hindu doctrines such as pure and pollution theories which ultimately alienates and reduces the Dalit masses to the bottom of the social pyramid."[23]

Since the psychological and religious dimensions of the Dalit Christian past and present may well hold the most important key to the Dalit Christian future, constructing Dalit Theology plays a crucial role in healing and empowering the Dalits.

Dr. Eaten Abraham, the first Indian Principal of the Serampore College, described the Dalits or Harijan, as they were beginning to be called by Mahatma Gandhi and from whom a vast majority of Indian Christians were drawn, as being the "Cinderella of the Nation', i.e., the rightful princes and heir to the throne being treated as servant maid within the Royal Household.[24]

---

[20] *Ibid.*, p. 27.

[21] *Ibid.*, pp. 27-28.

[22] K.C. Abraham, "Emerging Concerns in Third World Theology", *Bangalore Theological Forum* Vol. XXVI, No.3 & 4 (Sept and Dec, 1994) pp. 3-14.

[23] Aruldoss, *Why Dalit Theology?* p. 28.

[24] M. Azariah, "Doing Theology in India Today," in R. S. Sugirtharajah & Cecil Hargreaves (eds.), *Readings in Indian Christian Theology* (Delhi: ISPCK, 1995), p. 41.

Dalit Theology is unique since it deals with a particular people that are the Dalits. This is the theology of the Dalits, by the Dalits and for the Dalits.

> The Dalits are the victims and at the same time authors and originators of the Dalits theology. Moreover, it is articulated with the language and expression of the Dalits. It uses predominantly the stories, songs, proverbs, folklore of the Dalit people and interprets their history and culture with an aim to create a faith to live by and to act on their release.[25]

Good Dalit Theology–faithful to the Scripture and relevant to a particular cultural situation–cannot be done from a distance. The task of constructing Dalit Theology must be done in the context of worship and a right relationship to God and in the context of a commitment as Christ's disciples in His mission in that particular situation.

Another expression of Indian Christian Theology that would be relevant to the living situation of a vast majority of people in their widely dissimilar regions should be worked out to meet the requirements of Dalit Theology. A positive response to the situation can be found in constructing Dalit Theology that would be based on the living experiences of the Dalits themselves. It needs to take its roots from the actual realities or life experiences of the Dalits.

> 'Theology' is man's attempt and accomplishment in studying God including His attributes, action and accomplishment and His relationship with the created order including man, angel, nature, etc., systematically and academically. Since men differ from one another in terms of time, temperament, cultural background, circumstance thus they do not have uniform cognitive pattern, process, method, etc., when theologizing. As a result, there are numerous kinds of theology, for example, puritan and contemporary, liberation and feminist, Catholic and Protestant, etc. and multiple ways of theologizing, for example, biblical vs. historical, conservative vs. liberal, dispensationalist vs. reformed, etc.[26]

The need for theology is felt by Dalit Christians themselves. The constant humanlessness and bondedness actually pushed

---

[25] Aruldoss, *Why Dalit Theology?* p. 29.

[26] Wan, "Critiquing the Method of Traditional Western Theology and Calling for Sino-Theology."

them to create a theology of their own. They began to re-read and re-interpret the Scripture. According to James Massey, Dalit Theology really emerged during the 1980s. Prof. Arvind P. Nirmal, one of the pioneers of Dalit Theology, delivered an address in 1981 entitled "Towards a Sudra Theology" at Carey Society of the United Theological College, Bangalore. This address provoked a great deal of discussion and can be taken as the beginning of the evolution of Dalit Theology. "Dalit theology cannot be viewed only from the economic standpoint. The caste system and the institution of untouchability should also be investigated, since it becomes the primary cause of their poverty."[27]

The non-recognition of Dalit Christians in the Indian Church made them look for an alternative, and Dalit Theology eventually became the outcome to fulfill their aspirations. This shift in the realm of Indian Christian Theology became an inevitable and necessary alternative. Saral K. Chatterji, while speaking about the rationale for a Dalit theology, says, "The idea and ideology of caste as well as its morphological aspects, the nature of oppression, and the inherited inequalities perpetuated by it and its persistence through the interaction of social, cultural, religious and economic factors remained neglected in Marxian analysis."[28]

> This move implies a serious encounter with ethnic theological programs everywhere. The context of their belief, life and action must now be given priority."[29]
>
> The need for a theology is felt by Dalit Christians themselves. The constant humanlessness and bondedness actually pushed them to create a theology of their own. They began to re-read and re-interpret the Scripture. They began to perceive their history from a theological perspective. That was the reason for the emergence of Dalit theology. 'Theologians of every age are committed to interpreting the Gospel of Jesus in a way that is relevant and meaningful to the realities around them.'[30]

---

[27] Aruldoss, *Why Dalit Theology?*, p. 16.

[28] Saral K. Chatterji, quoted in K. P. Kuruvila "Dalit Theology: An Indian Christian Attempt to Give Voice to the Voiceless."

[29] J. Deotis Roberts, "Contextual Theology — Liberation and Indigenization."

[30] K. C. Abraham, "Third World Theologies", *CTC Bulletin*, May-December 1992, p. 5.

> The task of theologians and activities is to rewrite the theology and
> restore the original image. We need *Drista* (visionary), not *Jnata*
> (knower). All social codes, laws, customs and traditions derive their
> strength from religious scriptures as source. Theologians expected
> to provide hermeneutical principles for the decoding of the codes.[31]

Dalit Theology helps us in placing our past and present actions in a theological context. It will ultimately liberate by destroying the value systems that have contributed in making us captives. Dalit Theology is the Gospel of Christ.

Dalit Theology is important because correct doctrinal beliefs are essential to the relationship between the Dalit believer and God. One of these beliefs deals with the existence and character of God. Belief in the deity of Jesus Christ also seems essential to the relationship.

Source for Constructing Dalit Theology

Doing and developing Dalit Theology too requires the use of sources. There are probably many formative factors in the task of Dalit Theology. Some important factors that seem to call for special notice in the task, though they are not to be regarded as all on the same level, are discussed here. The sources and process of Dalit Theology lay in the anguish and affliction of the Dalits in their search for self-identity, equality and a meaningful life in the community and church.

Biblical Source for Dalit Theology

A clear grasp of and a genuine commitment to Dalit Theology, which seeks without reservation to be faithful to the Bible as the Word of God, is our first priority in attempting to develop Dalit Theology in the context of India and Hindu cultures. Scriptures dominate to bring the content of Dalit Theology to clear expression in words that embark us on the business of theology. John Macquarrie reminds us that just as the brain provides storage cells on which the memory of the individual depends, so "Scriptures or written

---

[31] Ravi Tiwari, *Reflections and Studies in Religion* (Delhi: ISPCK, 2008), p. 23.

revelation of God provide the people of Dalit theology a kind of memory by which it can reach back to and recall its past."[32] Scripture is the sole foundation of Dalit Theology.

Dalit Theology maintains close and positive relations with the Bible. We can get various sources for the task of Dalit Theology in the ministry of Jesus and the early Church including Paul and other apostles. Dalit Theology must keep in close touch with its biblical sources. But exclusion of non-biblical categories is meaningless here. There is no authentic Christian theology apart from this self-revelation of God in the Scripture.

Dalit theologians who have concertedly committed themselves to Dalit Theology should build their theology on the inspired and infallible Word of God, under the authority of our Lord Jesus Christ, through the illumination of the Holy Spirit. Their commitment should take seriously the historical and cultural contexts of the biblical writings.

The Old Testament

In the Old Testament, most of the prophets criticised and condemned the entire nation of Israel, but whenever they specified certain groups, it was always those classes or individuals in the country who wielded power, social, military or religious. Kings, priests, judges, generals and the rich fight against a prophet, Jer. 1:18; because they were the targets of their attack, Jer. 22:13-19; Mic 3:1, 9-12; Amos 5:12; Hos. 4:4-10. God heard the cries of the oppressed, Exo. 3: 7-9; 22:23-27.[33]

> The Old Testament prophets were inspired so intensely that they got the experience of a God who roars like a lion, Amos 3:8, rends like a wild beast, Hos. 13:7-8, says and blasts like a dynamite, Hos. 6:5; Isa. 9:8. The act of the God who avenges the poor on the

---

[32] John Macquarrie, *Principles of Christian Theology*, 2nd edition (London: SCM, 1966), p. 374.

[33] George Koonthanam, Yahweh the Defender of the Dalits: A Reflection on Isaiah 3:12-15, R.S. Sugirtharaj (ed.) Asian *Faces of Jesus* (New York: Orbis Books, 1993), p. 229.

criminal power-puffs is so really felt by the prophets in their proclamation that they with thorough matter-of-factness spoke of God coming directly to judge, Isa. 3:12-15; Mic. 6:1ff, Hos. 4:1ff. The more crushing the power structures were, the more vehement a prophet's attack on them was. In Israel, the pre-exilic period was witness to oppressive power amassed in a monarchical structure. The valiant and virulent pre-exilic prophets who denounced this tyranny of power are therefore rightly called the prophets of the golden age.[34]

The God whom Jesus Christ revealed and about whom the prophet Isaiah spoke is a Dalit God. God is a servant, the one who serves. Manu Dharma Sastra, the sacred law code of the Hindus, says that the Sudras (fourth Varna) were created by the self-existent to be servants of the Dvijas. The servitude of *varna* Dalits, placed below the Sudras, imposed on them as the rejected people is tragic and pathetic, beyond compare. It is easy to identify the Lord as the suffering servant of God in Isaiah's prophecy.

The New Testament

The synoptic gospels show that Jesus' concern for the poor and the outcast and His action for a different social order sprang from His direct, first-hand knowledge of His country, His people and the conditions in which they lived. Jesus associated with the poor, moved by preference in their circles, ate and drank with them, made their cause His own and sought to help them rediscover their own self and rebuild their pride, their faith and their power.

Jesus of Nazareth, the Lord of the Church, made His preferential option to the poor and the oppressed, namely the Galilean peasants, the publicans, the so-called sinners, the Gentiles, the Samaritans, the children and the women who were treated as outcastes of the society in Palestine 2,000 years ago. He had not only identified Himself with the disinherited and the rejected people of the society but had deliberately chosen to spend most of His three and half

---

[34] *Ibid.,* p.230.

years' ministry. He described them with great compassion as being "sheep without a shepherd" (Mark 6:34). He considered them "His own brothers and sisters" (Mark 3:34). And all the people who suffered conditions of deprivation like hunger, thirst, being naked and, as strangers, being sick and in bondage of all kinds as His own brothers and sisters whose suffering was so literally His own (Mt. 25:31-46).

> Christ's words and deeds attracted the Dalits very much and they became the ultimate model and pattern for their liberation. Jesus indeed became an awakener and conscientizer for them, which ultimately helped them to create a theology of their own in order to stimulate their kinsmen and to fight against all sorts of injustice done to them.[35]

His Nazareth Manifesto is really the manifesto for the Dalits. The gospel is for everybody. "It is precisely these people that the God of the Bible is primarily concerned with. Hence the Bible calls upon its readers, 'Open thy mouths for the dumb ... plead the cause of the poor and needy', Proverbs 31:8-9."[36]

The news of His birth was announced neither to the prince nor to the priests belonging to the upper strata of society but to the most despised shepherds of the Jewish society. Jesus' upbringing was in Nazareth, a tiny village in the region of Galilee, which was far removed from the centre of religion and economic power. It is nowhere mentioned in Scripture prior to his time, because it was an insignificant village. Further, Salvation is the result of participation in the liberation struggle. Christ frees us that we may free others. It is our task to observe where God is at work and to join in the liberation of the oppressed. Each must discover God in Christ at work where he or she is and move from that centre, being guided by the Spirit, towards making life more human. It is thus that we are set free as human beings both from the slavery of sin and the sin of slavery. It is thus that

---

[35] Aruldoss, *Why Dalit Theology?* p. 23.

[36] M. Azariah, "Doing Theology in India Today", p. 41.

we participate in liberation in order to uproot the systems of bondage—"that there may be no slaves or masters, but a co-humanity in Christ Jesus our Lord, in the church as an extension of the incarnation and consequently among all people."[37]

Like many Dalits, Jesus was also poor (Mt. 8:20). Apostle Paul expressed that Jesus, though he was rich, became poor for the sake of the masses (2 Cor. 8:7). As a son of a carpenter, Jesus belonged to the class of small artisans who were not at all rich. Like the Dalits, he was subject to physical and mental torture. He suffered hunger and thirst (Mt. 4:2; Jn. 4:6). Like many Dalits, he was considered illiterate (Jn. 7:15). His desert experience echoes the situation of the segregated Dalits. His death was another factor that asserts his Dalitness. Like the Dalits, he was left alone, scourged, spat upon, slapped and mocked. He was numbered among the robbers and hanged as a criminal. He endured terrible physical pain and crucified outside the city identifying himself with the outcastes of his day, Jn. 19:20.[38]

Both the biblical paradigms and the life of Jesus Christ became the motivating factor for the emergence of Dalit Theology.[39]

Pathos

Dalit Theology arises out of and bears testimony to the transformative power of the Christian Gospel. The *Missio Dei* concept has much in common with the kingdom of God motif. Harkness says that a redeemed society "is not identified with a reconstructed social order, though this may well be one of the demands of seeking God's kingdom and His righteousness."[40] Dalit Theology is an emerging

---

[37] Roberts, "Contextual Theology - Liberation and Indigenization."

[38] Aruldoss, *Why Dalit Theology?*, pp. 25-26.

[39] *Ibid.*, p. 26.

[40] G. E. Harkness, *Understanding the Kingdom of God* (New York: Abingdon, 1974), p. 54.

theology; it is in the process of developing in the realms of politics, economics, social structure and culture, as it has gained a powerful entry into sociological and theological writings. It is rightly remarked that "being an indigenous theology, it is more contextual and 'human-hood' praxis oriented."[41] The task of doing and developing Dalit Theology has also to do with communication of something that we believe to be universally relevant. It is the effective proclamation of the God-given message of salvation that is the actualisation of the message of Jesus Christ. We need to understand afresh our Dalit audience and preach the message in its entirety to them who are longing for God's intervention on their behalf. Thielicke comments that the "gospel must be put in modern terms. This is the only way modern people, including my neighbours, can assimilate it. Otherwise it will inevitably remain foreign to them."[42] This is very much true for the proclamation of the gospel to the Dalits as well.

A commitment to relevance will start with an awareness of the Dalits to who are communicating the gospel. Ken Gnanakan points out that "the prime objective of any theological methodology is to evolve a message that will be relevant to the people in real life situations and faithful to the Scriptures."[43] We are called and committed to listen, evaluate and be open-minded to different theological views in contextualisation, yet without compromise be faithful to the gospel and proclaim it in love. Gnanakan further remarks that in rendering the biblical message meaningfully, the interpreter needs to identify himself or herself with people in the plurality of their needs.[44] The task of Dalit Theology is to be carried on in the light of both the gospel and society,

---

[41] Aruldoss, *Why Dalit Theology?*, p. 1.

[42] Helmut Thielicke, *How Modern should Theology Be*, trans. H. George Anderson (Philadelphia: Fortress Press, 1969), p. 17.

[43] Ken Gnanakan, *Bible Theology in Asia* (Bangalore: Theological Book Trust, 1995), pp. 43-44.

[44] *Ibid.*, p. 266.

i.e., the contribution of various cultures, their sciences and arts, literature and religions.

> The task of theology is to discern 'signs' of God's presence and make that presence explicit or manifest. The internal factor that has contributed to the development of contextual theology is the shift in understanding of revelation. In traditional/classical theology, revelation is presented 'in the form of eternal truths handed down to us from Christ and the Apostles. Faith is understood to be the intellectual assent to those truths. All these are systematically arranged and presented as the... Faith.'[45]

There has also been a shift in the language of theology. In the past, the emphasis was on 'static continuities of human life.' The new language of theology emphasizes the 'dynamic aspects of human relationships.' This is consistent with the view about the inter-personal view of God's self-disclosure to the world. Instead of futile dichotomies which the old language of theology has engendered – nature vs. history, grace vs. law, individual vs. community, spiritual vs. material, etc.–the new language of theology affirms a holistic view of reality.[46]

Dalit Theology should affirm that the perspective of the oppressed is also the biblical perspective. To discern the voice of God in the poor is consistent with the revelation of God in the Bible.

Constructing Dalit Theology through Contextual Approach

The gospel is never an abstract truth but a message that takes concrete forms and continues to have dialogue with believers in their daily life situations. The product of such an enterprise is a Dalit theology that must be biblically oriented and response to the issues and challenges posed by the Dalits in India. As a pilgrim and prophetic community, God's people in India must continually pursue the hermeneutical task of relating God's word to the total Dalit

---

[45] Jose de Mesa and L. Wostyn, *Doing Theology; Basic Realities and Process* (Manila: Maryhill School of Theology, 1982), p. 80.

[46] Lourdino A. Yuzon, *Towards a Contextual Theology.*

context, discerning where the Holy Spirit is leading and being alert to the burning issues of the Dalits.

Developing Dalit Theology arises out of life experience and is inevitably rooted in the environment in which it is produced and articulated. It is to represent the spiritual journey of the Dalits who have to exercise their faith commitment as a minority among multiple religious traditions. The present part seeks to explore the lines theologising must take if it is to be fully contextual and truly responsive to the challenge of transformative action on the Dalit society. As Prabahkar says, "The task of theologizing by the Dalits will provide for them in their struggles the motivating force to liberate themselves, in solidarity with all other Dalits, across their religious and sub-caste loyalties."[47]

As Abraham Ayoorkuzhiel points out, "The aim of Dalit theology from a cultural point of view is to build up Dalit identity. Identity of a people results from the dialectics between structural and cultural systems."[48] The need for contextualising Dalit Theology has arisen because theology in the Indian Theological tradition has ignored Dalit issues.

Need for Contextualised Dalit Theology

Dalit Theology is facing a challenge to evaluate and to rethink the nature, the task of theology and the methodologies of theological construction in its own context. Dalit Theology is contextual. All theologies have emerged and reflected particular contexts in spite of claims to the contrary. Dalit Theology starts from an analysis and reflection of the Dalit context and seeks to interpret the Scripture in relation to this context. Christian theology is rooted in the event of incarnation; it needs to be rooted in the particular context of its emergence. As a report observes:

---

[47] Prabhakar, "The Search for a Dalit Theology", p. 201.

[48] Ayoorkuzhiel, "Dalit Theology: A Movement of Counter-Culture", p. 265.

> The contexts for theologizing are the authentic life experiences of
> these marginalized people, their struggles, their failures and
> successes, their conflicts and contradictions, their dreams and hopes,
> and their comradeship with people of other faiths and ideologies,
> etc.[49]

Like any other theology, Dalit Theology too needs the context. In the case of Dalit Theology, it is the Dalit context that is a living reality in the society that includes the Church or Christians. This first requirement plays a vital role in the formation of Dalit Theology to bring out the salient features of the life experiences of the Dalits. The emergence of Dalit Theology should be perceived in the context of Dalit search for identity and in relation to it.

Context of Dalit Theology

The context and backgrounds in which God's Word came to people during biblical times are very similar to the life situations of the Dalits today. The contemporary Indian context is characterised by the rise of Dalit consciousness. In Dalit Theology, analysis of the context is undertaken from the caste perspective. The methodology of Dalit Theology, which is the principle that governs the process of enquiry, analysis and evaluation, is caste. The Dalits are the ones who are exploited by the socio-economic traditions of this country. They painfully experience impoverishment and bondedness. Dalit Theology should come out of the experiences of the Dalits.

> The caste system which is the unique social system which is
> pervasive and has been primarily responsible for the oppression and
> dehumanization of the many. It can be boldly affirmed that no
> theological method is adequate if it does not recognize caste as the
> contextual reality and a major structure of oppression.[50]

The Church in India should develop Dalit Theology under the present political and social situation. Indian evangelicals

---

[49] Report of Group II in Social Action Groups and the Churches in India–A Consultation, Bangalore, CISRS, 1984.

[50] Devasahayam, "Doing Dalit Theology", p. 271.

need to respond to the current political situation theologically. The proclamation of the gospel message must reach the Dalits as well. As William Madtha comments:

> Dalit theology is born out of a live experience of the suffering or marginalized and their shared efforts to abolish their existing unjust situation and to build *basileia*; a new society, more free and more human, come what may. Hence, it is a theology of the riff-raff, the underside of history. Here the downtrodden become the historical *locus Dei*.[51]

The task of constructing Dalit Theology should facilitate the entrance of the gospel into Dalit culture and society. The task of doing and constructing Dalit Theology in their own Dalit context will bring a Dalit form of Christianity to the Dalits and the converts will accept it with all the Dalit trappings. Dalit Theology must be a confessing theology of the Word of God. It should enable the Dalits to understand the message well. D. S. Amalorpavadass observes:

> The Church in India needs a theology to understand the word of God, to realize what it means to announce Jesus Christ to our contemporaries, to make his announcement a meaningful and a joyful event, to render its content intelligible ...

Identity of Constructing Dalit Theology

The second most important aspect of contextualised Dalit Theology is the identity of the people with whom it is concerned. Just as Indian Christian theology deals with the identity of Indian Christians in their struggles and aspirations, Dalit Theology deals with the identity of the Dalits. Dalit Christians need to express their identity from their point of view.

New Thrust of Contextualising Dalit Theology

Constructing Dalit Theology requires new thrust by looking into the contextual life situation of the Dalits. "Dalit theology has been conceived in the context of struggles against casteism

---

[51] William Madtha, "Dalit Theology—Voice of the Oppressed," in James Massey (ed.), *Indigenous People: Dalits – Dalit Issues in Today's Theological Debate* (Delhi: ISPCK, 1994), p. 278.

and aspirations for social justice, both in the Church and society."[52]

"A commitment to God on one side and a commitment to their fellow Dalits who may belong to any religion, creed, ideology on the other, this dual commitment to solidarity is in a real sense the subject of Dalit theology."[53]

The new thrust in developing Dalit Theology should be concern for the sacredness of human life, injustice and freedom that finds support in the roots of our faith and so we need to rethink our traditional theological heritage that has largely remained indifferent to the distortions of our social system and political life and has attempted to confine our interest to personal piety and salvation of individual souls.

It is basically this concern about finding meaning for the suffering of all people and particularly the Dalits that an attempt is made to re-read and reinterpret the Bible from the perspective of Dalits in India. Dalit Theology should be true to the thrust of the total teaching of the Bible.

Task of Contextualised Theology

It is the task of Dalit Christian Theology to explain the experience of Jesus Christ that differs from other theologies, such as Tribal Theology and Urban Theology. It is the task of Dalit Theology to explore new modes and avenues of theological apprehensions so that the Christian message may be understood in the Dalit context. The task may find crucial text in doctrinal expressions.

"Dalit theology is diametrically opposed to classical theology that seeks to unravel not only the liberative and emancipatory meaning of the Gospel, but translates the hopes and aspirations of the Dalits in a given time, space and place."[54]

---

[52] Prabhakar, "The Search for a Dalit Theology," p. 203.

[53] Massey, "A Review of Dalit Theology," p. 9.

[54] Razu, "Contours and Trajectories of Dalit Theology," p. 41.

Major Problems in Contextualised Dalit Theology

The major problem in Contextualising Dalit Theology is that the theological task can be brought to a successful conclusion only by Dalit Christian theologians. Dalit theologians should join hands in carrying out this common task with Dalit anthropologists and philosophers. As Rajasekaran emphatically points out, "Christology should be the basis of Indian theology and not vice versa, because in Christian experience Christ is the central object as He is the Alpha and Omega, the Beginning and the End of it, it is applicable to the Dalit Christian theology also."[55]

Major theological subjects such as worship, sacrifice, cross, resurrection, indwelling operation of the Holy Spirit, revelation, Church, sacraments, sufferings and freedom in God should have fresh rethinking and searching analysis — a careful analysis to understand the finer aspects of Dalit aspiration for a restatement of our faith in the Dalit context and experience.

In the present situation, the proclamation of the gospel among the Dalits, the non-Dalit believer who shares the message with the Dalits and the Dalits who receive the message are involved in it. Consequently, the believing Dalits, who have the Dalit heritage, emerge into the scene. Now it is the role and responsibility of the Dalit believer to make the good news of the Lord Jesus Christ meaningful to the non-believers of their own community or to other community members. Here we should remember the words of V. T. Rajasekaran: "The task of theology now as in the past, on the one hand to maintain intact and unchanged the essence of the original given message and on the other hand interpret it to meet each fresh situation as it arises."[56]

Bishop Nirmal Minz states in his book entitled, *A Search for Common Ideology for Dalit-Tribal People*, that the struggle of

---

[55] V. C. Rajasekaran, *Reflections on Indian Christian Theology* (Madras: CLS, 1993), p. 100.

[56] *Ibid.*, p. 94.

the Dalits and tribals for their liberation includes liberation of humanity itself to become a casteless and classless society with justice and peace.[57] The biblical paradigm of the covenant of God with people provides a principle of contextual reinterpretation of Dalit reality in India.

Contextualisation of Constructing Dalit Theology

This theology should be relevant, contextual and contemporary so that it could be of value to the Dalits, the majority of the membership of the Indian Church today. Contextualisation of theology to suit the context of the Dalits plays a vital role here.

Sociological Foundation

Contextualisation plays a vital role in Dalit Theology. Dalit Theology should be contextualised in their own situations. For example, music, message, illustrations, counseling and every ministerial aspect should be based on their cultural and social context. But at the same time, it is the Word of God that examines the cultural and social aspects, never the other way. Contextualisation enables the people to discern and understand what God is saying to them.

It is more apt, as Robert J. Schreiter puts it, to speak not of universal, permanent and unchanging theologies, but of "local theologies."[58] God's encounter with the world through Jesus Christ takes place through the ordinary things of day-to-day life, which are transparent of God's presence. For instance, bread and wine used at the Lord's Table mediate to us the presence of the loving and living God who makes all things new. The world of things and all that "hath life" remind us of the creative power of God. If ordinary things are transparent of God's presence, then in the same way, we can speak of culture as something that is revelatory of God's presence. So, the continuing task of theology "is to

---

[57] Nirmal Minz, "Dalit-Tribal: A Search for Common Ideology" in James Massey (ed.), *Indigenous People* (Delhi: ISPCK, 1994). p. 140.

[58] Schreiter, *Constructing Local Theologies*.

reveal God's presence in a truly sacramental world."[59] A culture, whether "Christian" or shaped by other faiths, is not without witness to the presence of God in the midst of people.

The praxis model is not new. In fact, it continues the prophetic tradition that insists not only on words, but also on action, Amos, Isaiah, Jeremiah, Micah and the New Testament injunction to communicate in action the truth in love. It is also in keeping with the view that theology and ethics are inseparable.[60] The praxis model of contextual theology affirms the conviction that "truth is at the level of history, not in the realm of ideas."[61] Action is reflected-upon and reflection is acted-upon.

Contextualised Dalit Theology

Contextual Theology is an umbrella term. This is to say that there are many, not one, contextual theologies. For instance, Black Theology, Feminist Theology, Minjung Theology (Korea), Dalit Theology (India), theology of struggle (Philippines) and Latin American Liberation Theology are all contextual theologies that have emerged out of particular historical realities to which the liberative aspects of the Christian message are addressed.[62] The task of Dalit Theology should be ongoing in a context that demands an approach that should be comprehensive and interpretative for liberative praxis. Dalit Theology has the potential for breaking new grounds, so that its authenticity and contextuality be furthered by retaining its distinctiveness and connectivity.

Traits of Contextualised Theology

The principle of contextualisation indicates the situational character of Dalit Theology as it relates the text to the context.

---

[59] Bevans, *Models of Contextual Theology*,   p. 9.

[60] *Ibid.*, p. 65.

[61] *Ibid.*

[62] Yuzon, *Towards a Contextual Theology.*

The situational character of Dalit Theology in turn points to some marks of theological reflection. First, theological reflection serves a critical or prophetic function. The theologian or reflecting Dalit community should not only understand the biblical text in its original setting, but also relate it to the burning issues of the day. Through theological reflection, the Dalit community of believers analyses, judges and seeks to transform a given situation in the light of the biblical message.

In the task of contextualising Dalit Theology, indigenisation is a must. Thielicke further remarks that "when the Christian community in a place becomes conscious of its being the Church and fulfils the main task of *diakonia*, the church cannot but become indigenous."[63] There is a need to impart a more Dalit character to the outlook and customs of the church, while avoiding any dilution of the gospel or any blunting of its moral demands. Unless the Church understands the gospel in its context, she cannot proclaim to the Dalits meaningfully.

In the contextualisation of Dalit Theology, the Church and its theologians need to stand by Dalit women in solidarity, as they move forward in a rediscovery of their humanhood. Aruna Gnanadason observes:

> The Jesus community was basically a protest movement, rejecting accepted norms of relationship and behaviour. It was an egalitarian, not hierarchical community. The value system of the Jesus community developed under the hegemony of the poor. It offered love and acceptance to the suffering and poor outcastes — the scum of the society, including women.[64]

The Christian church in India, in a predominantly Hindu environment, has succumbed to the process of uncritical enculturation and is practicing caste in the lives of churches as well as Christians.

---

[63] Thielicke, *How Modern should Theology Be*, p. 17.

[64] Aruna Gnanadason, "Feminist Theology: An Indian Perspective," p. 70.

Significance of Contextualising Dalit Theology

Contextual or indigenous approaches to theological reflection in a localised situation are not restricted to the modern period.

> Developing the Dalit theology is also the most noble and impassioned of disciplines, as John Murray has noted, because its province is the whole counsel of God and [it] seeks, as no discipline, to set forth the riches of God's revelation in the orderly and embracive manner which is its peculiar method and function.[65]

> To speak of Dalit Theology is a liberative action in itself, considering that theology has been for too long the preserve of the elite, an academic discipline and an intellectual activity with little or no direct contact with realities experienced by people.[66]

Summary

Constructing Dalit Theology for Dalit liberation with a contextualising approach is exclusively for the liberation mandate of the Dalit Christians in India. Inherent in contextualising is the approach to the biblical text that gives serious attention not only to the life situation of the biblical writers and their original readers, but also to the faith-and-life situation of Dalit Christians. The biblical interpreter needs to be inside the context to render the text meaningful to the Dalits. Like Black Theology, Dalit Theology should emerge through efforts to reinterpret God's liberating presence in a society that consistently denies the Dalits their humanity, socially ostracizes them, economically exploits them and culturally subjugates them.

---

[65] John Murray, "Systematic Theology," in *The Collected Writings of John Murray,* Vol. 4 (Edinburgh: Banner of Truth Trust, 1982), p. 4.

[66] Mesa and Wostyn, *Doing Theology: Basic Realities and Process,* p. 80.

Chapter 5

Implications of Constructing Dalit Theology for the Liberation of the Dalits

Introduction

Dalit Liberation Theology intentionally articulated by present Dalit theologians is an outcome of the Christian Dalit Liberation Movement (CDLM). This was organised for Study of Religion and Society (CISRS) in the mid-1980s, with the goal of political action for raising Christian Dalits. CDLM is a national forum of Christian Dalit associations and groups that have existed in the country since the 1930s. For the past decade, CDLM has been developing both a theology and an ideology as a weapon and political strategy for taking appropriate action against the socio-economic and political oppression of Dalit communities.

This research will bring out some lessons for constructing Dalit Theology and its implications for the liberation of Dalit People in India. For this cause, Dalit consciousness should be understood by Dalit liberation theologians. It will also describe the nature, scope and purpose of Dalit consciousness and Dalit theologians' views of Dalit Christian history.

Towards Constructing Dalit Theology

The Dalits are those who are oppressed by the caste system in India. They account for about 16 per cent of the total population; they are discriminated against for being polluting or untouchable and are condemned to perform occupations such as leather tanning, scavenging, weaving and fishing—professions that are considered defiling and polluting.

Christian missionaries targeted the dominant caste groups to missionise and convert, and, when this failed, they began to evangelise the Dalits. Today, over 90 per cent of the church's membership in India consists of the Dalits.

Defining Dalit Theology

Though Dalit Theology is still experimental and tentative, James Massey, A. P. Nirmal, M. E. Prabhakar, A. M. A. Ayrookuzhiel and K. Wilson have arrived at some definite conclusion about Dalit consciousness as well as placing a value on missionary work. They claim that it was Black Theology, Liberation Theology and the secular Dalit consciousness produced by D P M that gave birth to Dalit Liberation Theology. They want Dalit Theology to be a liberation theology and have developed their theology after the pattern of their African and Latin American predecessors.

Dalit liberation theologians argue that since in the past, Indian theologians were upper caste people; they could not represent the experiences of the depressed classes. Ayrookuzhiel insists that Dalit Nationality is based on the Dalits' common experience of social and religious discrimination.

Dalit theologians advocate the total transformation of the entire Dalit society, whereas the missionaries preferred planting Christian congregations, building communities and erecting big churches. Dalit Theology is a theology of identity like Black Theology. Dalit theologians want Dalit Theology to emerge from the culture and traditions of the Dalits. John Webster observes that in many ways James Cone's Black Theology is relevant to the Dalits, in particular, the Scheduled Castes (SCs) of India.

There can be no common ideology for all Dalits, except on the basis of Ambedkarism. Therefore, Dalit theologians have decided to evolve a common ideology for the Dalits. They maintain that they have thus been attempting to bring together certain perspectives for Christian Dalits with a cohesive ideology.

Ingredients of Dalit Theology

According to James Massey, life-context, history and language are the three main ingredients for the formulation of Dalit Theology. Firstly, for Dalit theologians, the context has to be a Dalit context. Secondly, it must be based on the history, the content of the living stories of the Dalits. The third requirement is the use of the language of the masses in order to maintain their originality of thought.

Dalit Theologians' View of Dalit Christian History

Dalit liberation theologians contend that all people have a history and that the Dalits, particularly Christian Dalits, must be having a history as well. M. E. Prabhakar says that "as Dalits, they generally lack a sense of their common history, rich cultural heritage, and humanist traditions." Dalit theologians maintain that the history of the Dalits is the history of sufferings and struggles for liberation. The stories of their sufferings and protests are found in their folk songs, stories, myths, symbols and practices. Dalit liberation theologians have concluded that Christian conversion did not change the social status of the Dalits. They say that Christian conversion has, in fact, led to socio-cultural alienation. For Ayrookuzhiel, Christian Dalit Theology never forbids them from working with non-Dalit Hindus and Muslims in carrying out this mission

Scope and Purpose of Dalit Liberation

Dalit liberation theologians recently produced some theological literature on what they call Dalit Theology, which has been designed to awaken the consciousness of Dalitness among depressed class Christians. They were hoping that it would liberate or transform them from their present predicament of socio-economic and political oppression.

Gustavo Gutierrez also holds a similar view. Liberation means the oppressed becoming an awakened people and a new society. He contends that by this self-consciousness, the poor and the oppressed will gradually take hold of the reins of their own destiny. Consequently, the oppressed will realise their freedom and develop a new social order.

The above description shows, firstly, that the Dalit consciousness that has emerged from the articulations of Dalit liberation theologians is not primarily the consciousness of Indian people who are poor and oppressed. Secondly, for Dalit liberation theologians, Dalit consciousness is a combination of a socio-economic and political awakening of the Dalits and a new understanding of their history, religion and culture. Thirdly, for Dalit theologians, Dalit consciousness is counter cultural, that is, it is something unique and different rather than cross-cultural — something that confronts the two hundred years of Christian mission. The consciousness that emerged among the depressed class Christians was primarily cross cultural in nature rather than counter-cultural.

Dalit Liberation Theology

If Church authorities put the full might of the Church behind the Dalits, it is possible to bring about big socio-cultural changes in the country. For this, the Church must take to a new Dalit Liberation Theology and make it the principal mission of the Church.

In this new mission proposed for the Church, it has to take some precautions. No political party, not even a Dalit political party, will take interest in the social and religious liberation of the Dalits because that will affect their vote bank. That is why no party is taking a stand on this issue. Nor will the educated Dalit employees like it (of course, with minor exceptions). This is because, having taken advantage of reservations, they have been corrupted and co-opted by the ruling Brahminical Social Order. The Church has to conduct its social engineering experiment with the village-level Dalit organisations that still remain uncontaminated and revolutionary.

The ultimate function of Dalit Theology is two fold: to act in solidarity and to act for liberation. Liberation is envisaged as liberation of the Dalits from historically oppressive structures—both religio-cultural and socio-economic. So, theological articulation is not only a faith expression, but also a means for liberation. According to this school of thought, any theological expression that will not lead to action and the resultant liberation is futile.

The concept of solidarity has also emerged in this school of theology. Christian values of sacrifice, charity and commitment to others are all intertwined in this profound understanding of solidarity. Transcending his or her creed, ideology and religion, a Dalit is invited "to lose oneself for the sake of the other." Incarnational Theology is the basis of such a two-sided solidarity with God and with fellow Dalits. According to James Massey, the core of the act of the incarnation of God in Jesus was God's "acting in solidarity with human beings, particularly the oppressed of this world." Massey sees in this solidarity of God with human beings a challenge for Dalit solidarity: The model of solidarity we find in God's incarnational act in history challenges us Dalit Christians to follow it, so that the experiences we share with the Dalits in general should become the basis of an authentic Dalit Theology.

Being in solidarity with our fellow Dalits of different faiths and ideologies is a demand that the God of the Bible, through His own act of incarnation, places on Dalit Christians. This is an important factor for the authenticity of Dalit Theology, enabling it to become an instrument of destroying the social and religious structures responsible for the Dalits' historical captivity.

It is not merely the enslavement of the Dalits by the dominating groups that comes under the critical scrutiny of Dalit Theology, but also the enslavement of the Dalit psyche or "the inner nature of Dalitness." James Massey describes it as "a self-captivity" of the Dalit community. Dalit Theology seeks to liberate people from this slavery of "self-captivity," "a slavery from which it seems almost impossible to be liberated." The psychological dimensions within the Dalit theological movement are far more significant than we see at the surface. This should be recognised as an important aspect of Dalit Theology.

Theological Perspectives of Dalit Liberation

Dalit theological activity is mainly theological reflection, seeking the meaning of the present in the light of the history of God's redemptive acts and purposes. This produces a life-situation or pilgrim theology that arises from the necessity of confessing the faith in a changing Dalit socio-political milieu in which the Church is placed. Translating biblical truth within the Dalit situation involves what Filipino theologian Carlos Abesamis calls "bracketing off" the Western tradition of theology. To characterise Dalit Theology is to recognise its specific features, such as methodology, emphases, themes and concerns.

As William Madtha says:

> Dalit theology generates a revolution where all are equals as persons. This radical socialism humanizes human beings and leads them to the realization of the dictum: *Homo vivens, Gloria Dei.*

> It uproots the human tendency of 'having more' (*consumerism*) by fostering the tendency of 'being more' (*mysticism*). It transforms authority as service, (Mt. 20:28; Mk. 10:45; Lk. 22:27) ignoring status in society (Mt. 18:1-5; 20:20-28; Mk. 2:33-37; 10:35-45; Lk. 9:46-48, 22:24-27).[1]

The Dalit theological framework finds it shape most definitely in the initiating revelation of God. It must neither underemphasise the expectations that the interpreter brings to the revelation, nor negotiate the fundamental starting point in the construction of the theological framework. God must remain as the Lord.

Living Dalit Theology is the cutting edge between the Word and the world, and new world experiences of the Christians call for new theological reflections. While

---

[1] Madtha, "Dalit Theology - Voice of the Oppressed," p. 290.

"liberation" becomes a common, even popular word today, widely accepted in some theological circles, its basic theological meaning in Scripture should be sought. The deliverance of the Israelites from Egypt, from the land of bondage, is often seen as an example of liberation, where the afflicted and the oppressed were rescued by God from the power of enslavement and exploitation. So it warrants liberation until self-identity, freedom and independence. This understanding of the exodus in the Old Testament is conveniently adopted to advocate, support or justify certain reactionary movements in the present political and sociological scenes based on certain socio-economic, political ideology. This biblical event is understood in a socio-political perspective and interpreted from the context.

The praxis model of contextual theology is "basically sound." There are legitimate reasons for making this claim. As Bevans aptly puts it:

> The praxis model gives ample room for cultural expressions of faith, while providing exciting new understandings of the scriptural and older theological witness. In some ways, this model takes the concrete situations more seriously than any other model, since it regards theology not as a generally applicable, finished product that is valid at all times and in all places, but as an understanding of God's presence in very particular situations. There is certain permanence and even generality needed in the theological enterprise, of course, but the praxis model offers a corrective to theology that is too general and pretends to be universally relevant.[2]

The envisioning of the theological task is dependent on a renewed understanding of the role of the community in the life of faith. The contemporary situation demands that theology should not be viewed merely as the restatement of a body of propositional truths, as important as doctrine is. Gordon D. Kaufman rightly observes, "Theology is a constructive response to the community's affirmation that it is being impinged upon by the active presence of God."[3]

---

[2] Bevans, *Models of Contextual Theology*, P.71

[3] Gordon D. Kaufman, *In Face of Mystery: A Cognitive Theology* (Cambridge: Harvard University Press, 1993), p. 86.

Theology is home business within the community of Christians and from one member to another. Thus faith is the most essential prerequisite in the business of doing theology. Doing theology means to create, make or develop theology from the raw materials available. Obviously, it precedes studying or practicing

Christology of Dalit Liberation

The task of contextualising Dalit Theology for dalit liberation is to make the message of Jesus Christ intelligible and to make the choice for or against Jesus Christ inescapable. It should include the Christology that acknowledges Christ as the source and way, the heart and soul, the ground and goal of the task. When we contextualise Dalit Theology keeping Christology in mind, it helps us to take a fresh look at our Lord and Saviour Jesus Christ and to have motivation and direction in fulfilling the Great commission.

> The model for mission is His incarnation — identification without loss of identity, its cost is His cross — the seed which dies multiplies, its mandate is His resurrection — all authority is now His, its motivation is His exaltation the honour of His name, its power is His gift of the Spirit — who is the paramount witness, and its urgency is His parousia — we will have to give Him an account, when He comes.[4]

Theology and mission are inseparable, and a truly contextual Dalit Theology is one that empowers the Dalit church in mission. The authentic Dalit Theology must be grounded in mission and pastoral practice is absolutely vital. One distinctive characteristics of Dalit Theology should be its mission orientation. The Christian theological framework ought to be shaped by this ongoing concern for unity-in-diversity. The structural unity-in-diversity of the theological framework does not originate with the reader or with any system imposed on the text but with the unity-in-diversity of the divine and human authors of the biblical text. As Richard Gaffin has noted:

---

[4] John Stott, *The Contemporary Christian* (Leicester: Inter-varsity Press, 1992), p. 373.

> The biblical process is not heterogeneous, involving ongoing self-correction. Nor does it have anything to do with an evolutionary movement from what is erroneous and defective to what is relatively more and more true and perfect. The movement of the revelation process is from what is germinal and provisional to what is complete and final.[5]

The main thrust of New Testament Christianity was outreach. The Christian Church exists for mission and by mission. We should understand mission as meaning our total responsibility to the total person. Dalit Christians are constantly under pressure to reassert or to reject the lordship of Christ. It will be increasingly difficult for a mediocre faith to survive as outward pressures increase. The only way to survive is by aggressive outreach and creative mission.

The Gospel writers identified Jesus with the suffering servant of Isaiah. Since the service of others has been the privilege of Dalit communities in India, the Christology of a suffering servant is very much relevant in Dalit Christology. Therefore, to speak of a servant God is to recognise him and identify as a true Dalit deity. It may be mentioned that all people's theologies recognise this model of Christ as the servant in their Christology. Christ, the servant, is seen and affirmed in the faces of the poor.

Dalit God and Jesus the Dalit

Dalit theologians affirm that the Christian God is a Dalit god. This God, who is revealed in the Old Testament, and Jesus, who sided with the Dalits of the world, are the liberative paradigms for doing Dalit Theology. It helps them not only to come to terms with their historical consciousness, which is submerged in pathos and protest, but also to comprehend a God who in Jesus restores "humanness" to Dalits.

For Dalit theologians God is clearly a Dalit God. God, who reveals himself, both through the prophets and Jesus

---

[5] Richard Gaffin, "Systematic and Biblical Theology," *Westminster Theological Journal* 38 (1975-76), 289.

Christ, is a God of the Dalits. The servant God, a God who identifies with the servanthood of Dalits, is perceived by Dalit theologians as Dalit God. The servant role that the ex-untouchable played in India was indeed a participation in this "servant-God's ministries." Thus, Nirmal says, "To speak of a Servant-God, therefore, is to recognise and identify him as a truly Dalit deity.[6]

For Dalit theologians, Jesus is the ultimate Dalit, the servant God whom God reveals. However, it may be noted here that some of the recent theologians underplay the use of this servant imagery as it evokes extremely painful memories. Moreover, they feel, this will only help perpetuate structures of domination and subservience within which Dalits are caught up even now.

Jesus' tilt towards the poor and the marginalised, tax-collectors, prostitutes and lepers, according to Dalit theology, portrays Jesus as God incarnated as a Dalit. Devasahayam reflects as follows on Jesus' image from a Dalit perspective:

> Jesus reveals a free God, who is uncoopted and uncontained by those identified with religion This God is free to hear the cry of the outcasts against the guardians of religious society This God is not under the power of Brahman but is free to hear ones against Brahmans and other upper castes and side with the Dalits, who are ousted from the Temples and who are denied the right to study the Scriptures. The Cross has a special meaning in Dalit theology. Both the liberative praxis and the Dalitness of Jesus culminates in the symbol of Gurukul, 1992.'On the Cross, he was the broken, the crushed, the split, the torn, the driven-asunder man,' revealing his Dalitness.[7]

The vision of a new community under God is also envisaged by some Dalit theologians. Here the emphasis is on the invitation of Jesus to a new fellowship in which all participate equally and fully. "The focus is not merely on the oppression and God's option for the oppressed, but on the new

---

[6] Azariah, M. The Un-Christian side of the Indian Church: The Plight of the Untouchables Converts. Bangalore: Dalit Sahitya Academy, 1985 p.76

[7] *Ibid.*, p. 79.

community of freedom and fellowship, love and justice, which is the new people of the reign of God to which God calls all peoples.

Theologians like Wilson feel that God's plan is to transform the Dalits into a community that liberates not only themselves, but also their oppressors and so gives a liberative dimension to their very Dalitness.

The use of the Bible in Dalit Theology needs a special mention. Dalit theologians depend entirely on the Bible and Biblical examples. Dalit theologians are not essentially different from the liberation school of theology. However, there is a conscious and deliberate attempt on the part of Dalit theologians to re-read the Bible from the perspective of the experience of the victims.

Christian Contribution to Dalit Liberation

In Dalit Theology, analysis of the context is undertaken from the caste perspective. Their spirit is reduced or made faint due to oppression. Dalit Theology endeavours to discern God's action in the ongoing social struggles and turmoil. Dalits are the messianic community for they manifest messianic values that counter caste values. Dalits are the people who are bold to say, "Forgive our trespassers as we forgive those who trespass against us."

Christian faith is built on the Word's assumption of the body. Paul says that the process of new creation is characterised by groans against bodily violations while waiting for the redemption of the body. "And not only the creation, but we ourselves, who have the first fruits of the sprit, groan inwardly while we wait for adoption, the redemption of our bodies" (Rom. 8:23). Life in the sprit and freedom from the bondage are dependent on the redemption of the body.

> William Carey said of caste, 'it is the most cursed invention of the devil that ever existed; the masterpiece of hell.' Dr. Ambedkar referring to Christian Dalit says that in Hinduism his/her fall was

due to Karmas and in that Christianity it was due to ancestors' sin and therefore he was a sinner both at birth and rebirth.[8]

The cross seeks to dismantle caste consciousness, which makes the oppression of the Dalits possible. The cross must be seen as Christ's appeal to his disciples to join with Christ in Jesus' struggles against oppressive systems, through a transformation of our lives away from caste ideology as an authentic mark of our participation in the life and death of Jesus Christ. So, we shall interpret the cross as the reality that counters caste consciousness and highlight the nature of Dalit Theology as counter ideology.

Role of Conversion

The social and religious aspirations of the Dalits are not only to liberate themselves but through that to save India itself. According to Dr Babasaheb Ambedkar, the Father of India, who conducted a series of experiments in this field, this is possible only through religious conversion. Religious conversion is the best, the simplest, the most inexpensive and the most non-violent way of not only liberating the Dalits, but the country as a whole. It is as simple as that.

The upper castes (Hindus) give equal treatment to the Christians, the Muslims and the Sikhs. People belonging to these three sections (called religious minorities) did not come from outside India. Christians of India did not come from Rome, and Muslims did not come from Arabia. They are converts from today's SC/ST/BCs. They achieved equality and self-respect only through conversion. When 20 per cent of India (Muslim, Christian, and Sikh) could achieve equality and self-respect through such a simple act of social engineering (conversion), why cannot the rest of the SCs/STc/BCs follow this simple path?

Never-ending Caste War

Such a conversion will bring happiness to the SCs/ST/BCs as well as their oppressors (Hindus). As long as the Dalits

---

[8] (Speech delivered by) Dr B. R. Ambedkar: *Why Go For Conversion?* Dalit Sahitya Academy, reprinted 1987, p. 35.

remain within the Hindu fold, they have to fight with the Hindus daily. See what happened in Jhaj jar (Haryana) recently. It is a daily fight in the countryside today. India is full of caste wars between the Hindus and the Dalits. Conversion will once and for all end this war and violence, and there will be peace in the countryside and India as a whole.

The Hindus may ask: When there is caste inside the religions of Muslim, Christian and Sikhs, why again go into such a leaking house? This is a mischievous question. There is a great deal of difference between the Hindu caste system and the castes within other religions. Caste is not the chief characteristic of these religions. But the Hindu caste system has religious sanction. Even M. K. Gandhi, the father of the Hindu nation, defended the caste system because it had the blessings of Hindu religion. That is why no Dalit has been made a Shankarachari to this day. But several Dalits have become Bishops, Imams, and Sikh Saints. They can destroy their castes without destroying their religions. However, if you destroy the caste system, Hinduism itself is dead. This is because the caste system is the other name for Hinduism. Kill caste, and Hinduism is dead.[9]

Role of Christians

Brahmin Chief Minister Jayalalita brought a new law in Tamil Nadu with the same reason—to see that the Hindu edifice does not crumble and become a minority religion. But none of these legislations or state-sponsored tyranny can stop the oppressed people from seeking social justice. That work is going on—silently but steadily.

The leadership of Muslims, Christians and Sikhs can speed up this process of social justice through conversion. Islam does not have the machinery for conversion. Christians have their powerful evangelical wing. But after the foreign

---

[9] Rajasekar V. T., Weapons to fight Counter Religion, Dalit Sahitya Academy, 2004, p. 100.

missionaries left India, the work in this direction slowed down, if not almost stopped. This is because upper-caste Christians captured church leadership and did not want to hurt their cousins in the Hindu ruling class. Had the church leadership launched a powerful struggle, the Government of India would have been forced to withdraw the 1950 Presidential Order.

Dalits Betrayed

The Church leadership betrayed the Dalits who would have simply flocked into Christianity (at least in South India) had the Presidential Order been withdrawn. The Church leadership, both Protestant and Catholic, did not look at the Dalit issue beyond its selfish interest, that is, beyond conversion.

The Church is not interested in liberating the Dalits as a whole. The persecution, daily struggle, the rampant racism in the countryside, young Dalit girls becoming prostitutes, their hunger, unemployment, murder and mayhem—their struggle for social justice—does not interest the Church. What type of church is this?

Today's Dalits, the worst persecuted section of society, are in a very bad shape: They are totally impoverished. We are not referring to the SC/ST people enjoying the reserved jobs. They form just 2-3 per cent of the Dalit population. The village-dwelling, illiterate Dalits are on starvation diet. Poverty and deprivation are not giving them even a chance to think. A revolution is preceded by a revolutionary situation. Such a revolutionary situation is not existing in any part of India.

A hungry man cannot be a revolutionary. So, an organised religion like Christianity has the ability to create a revolutionary situation among the Dalits by supporting their socio-economic needs and then by awakening them. As the Bible says, "Know the Truth and Truth shall make you free."

Change in the Attitude of the Church

Did the Church tell the truth? Did the Church identify the enemy? The poor, innocent Dalits do not know who their enemy is and who their friend is. Once they come to know the truth, they will simply explode. Why has the Church failed in its most important duty towards the oppressed?

The upper-caste church leadership is not taking an interest in such activities. Had this leadership taken liberation of the Dalits as the sole objective of the Church, the non-Christian Dalits would not have opposed the Dalit Christian reservation issue.

Lately, the attitude of church leadership changed a little bit. The Church offered full support to the Dalits' case before the United Nations Conference at Durban, which sought to equate India's casteism with racism. India's upper-caste-led government vehemently opposed our demand and defeated us at Durban, though for the first time, the world was shocked to hear about the horrible Hindu apartheid system prevailing in India. After Durban, we find a welcome change in the attitude of the Church.[10]

Dalit Christians

The Church can embrace the Dalits only if it gets the full cooperation from its own Dalit Christians, who form over 60 per cent of the Christian population. Unfortunately, Dalit Christians are angry with the Church. When the upper castes within the Church are not treating their own Dalit Christian brothers as equals, how will the Dalits outside develop a trust in the Church?

There is a lot of mistrust between Dalit Christians and the Dalits. This can be removed if the Church gives a prime place to Dr Ambedkar's revolutionary thoughts and accords a prime place to the "Father of India." It can also seek the cooperation of Muslims in this task.

---

[10] Azariah M., The Un-certain side of the Indian Church –The Plight of the Untouchable Converts, Dalit Sahitya Academy 1989, p. 55.

India's second independence struggle for social and religious liberation is possible only if the Daiits are at the forefront of this movement. The Dalits are willing. They are impatiently waiting. The Church—being the most well-organised, cadre-based organisation, with millions of its dedicated sisters working in every corner of India—is ideally cut out to act as a catalyst for such a revolution. Is the Church ready?

Towards a Dalit Liberative Hermeneutics

Roots of Dalit Liberation

In their struggle for identity, the Dalits have emerged as the strongest force in India today as ever in history. Nearly 200 million Dalits in general and 15 million Dalit Christians among them are active subjects of this great history of India today.

As the struggle of the Dalits is on to regain their lost identity, the issues related to this struggle are not new. Christian Dalits are part of this struggle with additional problem of caste and hierarchy in the Church. In view of this, Dalit Christians in particular are on the genuine lookout for some of the religio-cultural and theological resources that would directly address to heal their wounded psyche.

Since their problems are notched up with several unjust systems and structures both within and around their church situation, they are on a serious search for their liberative and praxis-oriented resources available in and around the Bible, which stands as the centre of their religious fervour. If the Dalits are seeking their liberation from casteist oppression, and to identify their religio-cultural energies from a religious and social base for their corporate and individual attempts at liberation, the Bible stands as a dynamic source of energy. The present study attempts to re-read the Bible in the light of the Dalit hermeneutical focus. The Psalms of Lament are used as a fertile ground on which the quest for Dalit liberative praxis can be sufficiently planted. In this venture, two things are done specifically: Firstly, situating the Psalms of Lament in their original setting (if at all that is possible) for a meaningful appropriation of their message; and secondly, appropriating the interpretative keys available with the Psalms to resonate and to discover the liberation potential that is in convergence with Dalit liberation. In order to venture into this task, a few methodological observations need to be made at this point.[11]

Methodological Observations

For any critical and constructive engagement of Dalit liberation with biblical resources, we need to take note of the following important methodological observations that will enhance the process of our interpretation:

- The issue of common ground between the biblical world and Dalit world is of paramount importance for any heuristic exploration of either of these areas and to see their integral interconnection. The struggles of the Dalits can easily find a natural affinity towards the struggles and experiences of the marginalised communities of the Bible written down as the faith expressions in their various traditions. In other words, there are certain points of convergence in the matrices of the biblical and Dalit worlds.[12]

- Liberative hermeneutics is the common ground and concern in our quest to see inter-relatedness between the biblical and Dalit worlds. The important objective in the liberative praxis for the Dalits is their liberation from socio-cultural oppression. The Dalit liberative praxis-oriented hermeneutics is geared towards the liberation of the Dalits from psychological, cultural and social oppression and to empower them to get organised in their struggle for freedom. It is this understanding that should percolate the context of the oppressed communities of

---

[11] http://. www. Religion-online.org/show article.asp 2008-12-09

[12] *Ibid.*

the Dalits in India as they search for human experience of God in and through their socio-cultural milieu.

- In the light of the above two criteria set out for the common ground of interpretation for both Dalit liberation and biblical foundation for that purpose, certain new textual stirrings have been noted in the Indian interpretation of the Bible.

The other major concerns surfacing in this process are the orality and literacy of the text, God as an active agent of the poor and the marginalised and the vulnerability of God alongside sovereignty. These issues will naturally let us move into our ground reality of considering the issue of Dalit hermeneutics.

Dalit Hermeneutics for Liberative and Praxis-Oriented Exegesis

In order to engage ourselves in Dalit hermeneutics for liberative and praxis-oriented reading of biblical texts, it is necessary that we clearly set our goals and objectives. While this task is not radically different from what we do in biblical hermeneutics, the interpretative principles are similar to some extent in both. However, Dalit hermeneutics is dalit-context-specific with clear-cut defined objectives and goals. It seeks to read the texts in transaction with grassroots and other subaltern communities who may have inherited a similar methodology.

While these general functions are in order with the Dalit hermeneutics for liberative and praxis-oriented purposes, the specificity of its function can be seen in different ways.

Firstly, by using the hermeneutics of "suspicion", "retrieval" and "representation", Dalit hermeneutics seeks to concentrate on the integral liberation of Dalits themselves. Some of the key interpretative questions raised by scholars or people who are engaged in Dalit hermeneutics are well summarised by A. M. Raja:

> Are the actual and official preaching from the pulpits or platform vibrating with the biblical claims of God's bias in favor of the people thrown to the periphery? Would the eschatological promise of the biblical texts be the mesmerizing agents in persuading the Dalits to forget the present phase of apparently inconclusive pain and suffering due to oppression? Is biblical orientation otherworldly? Is the jubilant song of the exodus people after crossing oppressive Egyptian boundary, a meaningless composition? Could the "silence" of Job in the thick of wretched conditions, be the source of inspiration for activating the legitimate wrath of Dalits against their enemies? Should the suffering servant of God nakedly crucified in public be the model of liberation to the Dalits who are "crucified" day in and day out, openly and subtly?[13]

To these areas of interrogation of the diverse trajectories of the Bible, we could even add: Can the agonising and anguishing moments of the faith of Psalmists be hidden in and around their destiny? Has the rule of Yahweh come and out broken to change the existing situation? Who are the evil people, people of violence and people of tongue who can cause so much damage to the reputation of the Psalmists, even to their very existence? How about the advocacy of the Psalmists who show favoritism towards the poor and weak, who are crushed at the gate of justice? (Cf. Psalms 41:1-2; 82:3-4). These questions are well within the operation of hermeneutics of suspicion employed by Dalit Christian readers of the Bible when they are brought into a direct encounter with the latter. At the same time, Dalit readers of the Bible should not ignore the fact that there is a tremendous liberation potential available with the Bible for transformative and performative functions

Thus, both the hermeneutics of suspicion and retrieval are equally helpful for the Dalit hermeneutical task when it engages in dialogue with the biblical text.

Secondly, Dalit hermeneutics is also the net result of bringing to the fore the glaring social reality of the caste system (*Varna* of the Hindu religious tradition) and from

---

[13] Arvind P.Nirmal, "Doing Theology from a Dalit Perspective", p. 140.

there it proceeds to work out a hermeneutics based on the principle of equality. It is also the net result of disentangling the biblical text from its firm entanglement with "high culture" and caste Christians.

If the biblical text has to become a tool or vehicle of emancipation, Dalit reading of the Bible has to take its liberative and egalitarian potential in all its parts. This is helpful not for Dalits alone, but for all the readers of the Bible. In this sense, Dalit hermeneutics has to serve to bring out a counter culture against the oppressive caste culture and it further questions the dominant traditions of Hindu philosophy and Brahminical Indian Christian Theology as well as the ambiguous missionary reading of the biblical texts, which seems to legitimise the status quo. This necessitates in not only opting for a methodological exclusivism of Dalit hermeneutics, but also creating a counter epistemology, which is against caste hierarchy and missionary subtlety; but in tune with Dalit liberation and struggle.

Thirdly, Dalit hermeneutics also shares in common some of the relevant concerns on par with any liberation hermeneutics for contemporary exegesis and various processes related to it. Biblical hermeneutics is the source of interpreting the texts, especially of their past history, whose original meaning is no longer immediately available to the present in the light of their present experience. So hermeneutics has two eyes: one before and the other behind. With the "eye behind", it looks back to the experiences of God's people, Israel, their creedal confessions and even the retelling of their own traditions. This process will help us to be clear about the historical biblical context. With the "eye before", hermeneutics looks to the present. It discovers the challenges of current social and historical reality. It further tries to make an integral connection between faith and life, between the loving actions of God in the past in the realm of Israel's faith and the present socio-economic and cultural reality.

J. L. Segundo articulates this dialectics when he writes:

> It is the continuing change in our interpretation of the Bible which
> is dictated by the continuing changes in our present day reality,
> both individual and social. So, the Bible has its specific role in it.[14]

Fourthly, Dalit hermeneutics takes a serious note of *intertextuality*. By this, we mean the biblical texts should be in constant dialogue with the "living stories" and "concrete experiences" of the Dalits. For instance, the stories of Dalit martyrs and the stories of Biblical martyrs can be matrixed to find common elements in both for an integral Dalit liberation.

The process of intertextuality also summons us to think in terms of orality of the scripture, "oral traditions" and "orally transmitted" stories of the Bible, which speak of their fluid and flexible intertextual participation in their faith and liberation journey. Therefore, one needs to think about the transformative and liberative purposes of the Dalit Hermeneutical inquiry, which is at its heart.

Analysis of Dalit Theology for Dalit liberation

In Dalit Theology, analysis of the context is undertaken from the caste perspective. Their spirit is reduced or made faint due to oppression. Dalit Theology endeavours to discern God's action in the ongoing social struggles and turmoil. The Dalits are the messianic community for they manifest messianic values that counter caste values. The Dalits are the people who are bold to say, "Forgive our trespassers as the forgive those who trespass against us."

Christian faith is built on the Word's assumption of the body. Paul says that the process of new creation is characterised with groans against bodily violations while waiting for the redemption of the body. "And not only the creation, but we ourselves, who have the first fruits of the spirit, groan inwardly while we wait for adoption, the

---

[14] http://www.sbl-site.org/publicationarticle.asp.2008-12-09

redemption of our bodies" (Rom. 8:23). Life in the spirit and freedom from the bondage are dependent on the redemption of the body.

William Carey said of caste: "It is the most cursed invention of the devil that ever existed; the masterpiece of hell." Dr. Ambedkar, referring to Christian Dalits, says that in Hinduism, his or her fall was due to *karmas* and that in Christianity, it was due to ancestors' sin and so he was a sinner both at birth and rebirth.

The cross seeks to dismantle caste consciousness, which makes the oppression of Dalit possible. The cross must be seen as Christ's appeal to his disciples to join with Christ in Jesus' struggles against oppressive systems, through a transformation of our lives away from caste ideology as an authentic mark of our participation in the life and death of Jesus Christ. Thus, we shall interpret the cross as that reality that counters caste consciousness and highlights the nature of Dalit theology as counter ideology.

Aims and Objectives of Dalit Theology for Dalit Liberation

* To create awareness among the people, especially the Christians, about Dalit realities and to make them respond to concrete situations

* To make people understand Dalit Theology and biblical foundations

* To promote Dalit liberation education among Dalit Christians

* To organise people for struggles against Human Rights violation and atrocities

Dalit Theology recognises emotion as an important human dimension and so also a language because of the subject matter—the pathos and hopes of the Dalits as well as the passionate commitment of thinkers for Dalit liberation.

Future Directions for Liberation of the Dalits

(1) Dalit Theology is part of the postcolonial struggle of different communities for their distinct identity and space. In a largely homogenising trend influenced by two processes , namely globalisation and Hinduisation, Dalits and Dalit Christians are still struggling for a Dalit identify of their own. Intra-Dalit conflicts and Dalit sub-groups still continue despite the striving for a common Dalit identity and solidarity. Therefore, the challenge for Dalit Theology is to strike an ideal balance.

Hindutva revival or reform movements are trying to absorb Dalits into a monolithic Hindu fundamentalist culture. Their systematic propaganda concentrates on the message that Dalits had been truly part of the "Hindu" religio-cultural structure. Several Hindu organisations are involved in re-conversion efforts to drive home this ideology. Although it is a clear historical distortion, the Dalits are caught up in a dilemma whether to declare their solidarity with the Hindus or the Dalits. In fact, the Dalits are caught between Hinduisation and Dalitisation. This historic dilemma appears to have had its impact upon Dalit Christians and Dalit theological movement too. This may be the reason why this new strand of theology appears to be at a standstill right now.

However, the recent effort to genuinely develop a constructive theological strand is a welcome change. The trendsetting work of Sathiyanathan Clarke, *Dalits and Christianity Subaltern Religion and Liberation Theology in India* (1998), deserves special mention here, as it opens up new avenues for the Dalit Theology movement.

(2) The almost total dependence on biblical thought for theological construction needs further reconsideration in the light of the historical experience of the Dalits.

Pre-existing or Christian egalitarian thoughts and struggle for equality and justice were evident in Dalit history and memory But the early Dalits had their own ways of protest and resistance. This is ignored by Dalit theologians.

Dalit theologians also need to widen the definition of "texts," given the oral emphasis on Dalit tradition By probing into Dalit folklore and songs, they are likely to unearth extra textual sources for doing Dalit Theology. This could also help create new hermeneutical principles unique to Dalit theological movements.

(3) Ancestral worship and female deities appear prominently in Dalit myths and songs. Dalit theologians could explore how the pre-existing religio-cultural ideas might have shaped their journey into Christianity and how they deal with such questions in their everyday life. All these could function as a rich source of theologising and Dalit faith articulation in India.

(4.) While pathos, suffering and pain have found a place in Dalit Theology, the rich Dalit traditions of celebrating life in the context of communitarian values seem to have been completely forgotten by Dalit theologians with a few exceptions. The rich culture of the Dalits has a lot of egalitarian ideas. This needs to be further explored by Dalit theologians.

(5) The "dialogue" and "accommodation" that take shape at the popular level of both Hinduism and Christianity need a systematic consideration by Dalit Theology. It appears that in a silent way, people at the village level are moulding meaningful "systems" of interaction in a pluralistic socio-religious setting like that of India. If "the reality of the religion of a people can be studied only through the empirical enquiry into the meaning appropriated by them as persons and community of persons in their life situations," then Dalit Theology needs to look carefully into the popular level of Hindu-Christian religious encounter. Luke and Camian's study reveals that religious boundaries at the level of belief systems and rituals are not so marked in the minds of the people in villages. In the popular worship context, there is

mutual sharing of practices, symbols and values without so much fuss. These marginalised spaces deserve systematic attention.

Western Christian theology is highly individualistic and does not take history, especially that of the oppressed, seriously. What marks Dalit Christian Theology out is the centrality it gives to the question of caste and caste oppression, which is unique to India. Caste is an important category in Dalit Christian Theology in analysing social oppression. This should be seen in the light of the fact that the leaders of the Indian Christian Church sought to convince its own members that everyone is equal in Jesus Christ, despite the existence of gross discrimination against the Dalits inside the Church itself. What Dalit Theology began to do was to force the Church to recognise this discrimination and oppression of Dalit Christians

Reflection: What Is Dalit Theology Going to Do for Dalit Liberation?

The emergence of Dalit theology in India can be considered as a significant event in the history of Indian Christian thinking, as it is very much related to the historical experiences of an oppressed and downtrodden people. It can be conceived in the context of the struggles of a community against casteism and their continued aspirations for social justice both in the Church and society. However, the immediate concern for formulating Dalit Theology emerged within the Christian Dalit Liberation movement. So, the sources and process of Dalit Theology lay in the agony and sufferings of the Dalits in their search for self-identity, equality and meaningful life in the community. K. C. Abraham, President, Ecumenical Association for Third World Theologians, rightly points out: Dalit Theology emerges out of the attempt in their seeking a new identity for themselves based on their past religions and cultures which had been suppressed or destroyed by dominant communities. In their struggle against historical and contemporary process of domination, the Dalits and indigenous groups became conscious of their identity as people

Dalit Theology is an indigenous theology, as it is emerged out of the Indian context and out of the self-generated and self-directed Dalit consciousness. While Indian Christian Theology has failed to take account of the sufferings and hopes of the Dalits, Dalit Theology arose as a counter-theology to fulfill the aspirations of the Dalits. It became a critique to oppose the principles and practices of casteism and the institution of untouchability, which are rooted in the religious traditions of Hinduism and defended under the shadows of Hindu doctrines. This theology criticises and questions Hindu doctrines, which alienate and condemn the Dalits to the bottom of the social pyramid. Dalit existence is characterised by a·sense of powerlessness and so Dalit theology's priority is with the task of empowerment. This empowerment is irrevocably linked to the mission of establishing the kingdom, and theology should encourage people to involve themselves in struggles for a just society. Dalit Theology should continuously keep the hope of Jesus' return to power alive, which gives meaning and significance to Dalit struggles. This is part of the general awakening of the broader Dalit community.

Dalit Theology has been intertwined with the lives, experiences and struggles of the Dalits. So, the message that was put across very forcefully was that a genuinely Indian Christian theology was not simply about celebration and joy, but also rooted in the sufferings of the Dalits. Dalit Christian theology challenges the structures of the status quo, both within as well as outside the Church, which are primarily casteist. That is its prophetic function based on what we believe that the Church should be. This is the task of unveiling the structures of power that are putting on a mask of neutrality to hide the operation of caste within the Church but are still using the power of caste in ways that are unjust. Dalit Theology has another important role: Empowering Dalit communities to reclaim their position in a way that could lead them to bring out their own experiences and express them in their own symbolic modes. This would add strength to their struggle for empowerment and for a more equal distribution of power and resources. This is actually happening today, through a networking of many resistive forces, of which Dalit Christian Theology is one. Dalit Theology, which is taking shape in India, can be considered as one of the attempts to do a local theology taking seriously the context of struggles of the people who are marginalised and oppressed, reflecting on their struggles for liberation from the structures that marginalise them. It is very much committed to the liberation and humanisation of the Dalits, the most oppressed of India. It is understood as the systematic reflection on the liberating and humanising actions done by and on behalf of the oppressed, which becomes the mediation as well as the sacrament of God's saving action in history. Its concern is not mainly what would happen to the soul after death, but what happens to the human being to have their human dignity and honour as anybody else.

Dalit Theology not only shows a relevant perspective for doing a local theology, but also questions the so-called neutral philosophical perspectives of theology. It exhibits its conflict with the elite perspective, which justifies the status quo that leads to exploitation and oppression.

Dalit Theology is a "theology from the underside of history" This means that it is based on the discernment that the theological reflection should be done from the perspective of those who are victims of domination and oppression. It is clearly an attempt to give voice to the voiceless of the Indian society. This is why it provides a paradigm for assessing the signs of the times. The irruption of the poor and the oppressed is one of the greatest signs of the times. It is also the time of the irruption of God in history to establish his reign and righteousness. Needless to say, no theology can be done today ignoring the signs of the time.

This is not a theology created by the intelligentsia, the affluent, the powerful or those on the top. It is a theology from the bottom, from the underside of history created by the victims, the poor and the oppressed. It is not a theology spun out in a series of principles of timeless truths that are applied to the contemporary scene, but a theology springing out of poverty, oppression, the heartrending conditions under which the great majority of Latin Americans live.

Moreover, Dalit Theology affirms the biblical faith that the poor are today's suffering servants, today's "crucified peoples." Their suffering sheds light on the evil and injustices prevalent in religion and society and condemns them. Their struggle for a full human life and dignity announces the hope of a new world, the redeemed humanity. Despite the fact that the Dalits are India's suffering servants and crucified people, their theology calls for an "obligatory solidarity" with the poor of the whole world, a necessary task in doing theology today.

Dalit Theology as a local theology differs very much from missionary theology, which is evangelistic in nature and aims at the conversion of Dalits to Christianity from their original religion. The teachings of the missionaries in India provided only half the salvation to the Christians. It was a half salvation, as in it no effort was made to relate the teachings of Christian faith to the real life of the people. But Dalit Theology seeks to help the Dalits to live in solidarity with their fellow Dalits despite the religious background. Since it assumes religious pluralism of our context, it not only helps Christian Dalits, but also shares a common ideology with other Dalits in their common struggle for liberation, justice and dignity.

Further, Dalit Theology shows a radical discontinuity with the Indian Christian Theology of the *Brahmanical tradition.* In this case, Dalit Theology is a counter theology in relation to other dominant theologies. The dominant theologies are considered to be normative and so imposed upon the oppressed. As the Brahmanic theological tradition is a dominant tradition, it has been imposed upon the Dalits, who are the Christian majority.

The ascended humanity of Jesus is the pledge of the consummated destiny of the oppressed, because Jesus suffered as a representative of the oppressed collective. The oppressed have a right, rather a duty, to ascend. "Let us run with perseverance the race that it set before us, looking to Jesus, the pioneer and perfecter of our faith, who for the sake of the joy that was set before him, endured the cross, disregarding its shame, and has taken his seat at the right hand on the throne of God."   Amen

Conclusion

The Dalits have the right to life and live life to the fullest. This is promised under Dalit Theology. All along, the Brahminic forces have created powerlessness among the Dalits. Exclusion to the highest level has been firmly established. Now under Dalit Theology, a space is created for the Dalits into the realisation of their being as human beings.

Theologically speaking, Dalit Christians were no longer Dalits. Instead, they were part of the servant people of God, a community with resources to help, committed to function as God's leaven in Indian society as a whole. The Christian community would play this role not by functioning as a self-serving political bloc in the competition for "loaves and fishes" but by bringing the teachings and dynamic of Jesus to bear through its members on all aspects of Indian life.

The Dalit God also shares the pathos of the Dalit people and provides the healing they need to carry on their struggle as well as to realise their full humanity. God calls Christian Dalits to participate actively and even lead in the grassroots political struggle of all Dalits for the liberation God intends. In that struggle, the Church has proven to be weak, ineffective and often as an instrument of caste oppression, even though it is predominantly Dalit in composition. The Church must repent and become the shalom community God created it to be, living and acting in solidarity with all the Dalits.

Dalit Theology runs counter to the existing Indian Christian theology, which has been articulated mostly by upper-caste theologians who they claim ignored the interests of the Dalits. It is an Indian version of liberation theology and seems to take the course of Black liberation theology. It is doing theology in community within the contexts of the sufferings and struggles of Dalits through dialogues, critical reflection and committed action for building a new life-order.

Each generation has left its own unfinished business and unaddressed issues for the next to deal with. Those who are shaping the great theological tradition *vis-à-vis* Dalits in India today are no exception. Their agenda includes interacting theologically with the little theological traditions of Dalit Christians, with other theological traditions within the Indian Church and with the Dalits who do not share their Christian convictions.

Dalit Theology should be periodically updated in order to establish liberty and security as Dalit rights. The state will have to look beyond the existing legal system, into the social dynamics of caste forces and enact legal safeguards in favour of the Dalits, women and other downtrodden peoples. Contextualised Dalit Theology has a historical context, a contemporary context and an eschatological context. An appropriate contextualisation of Dalit Theology leads to the holistic emancipation of the Dalits. It announces good news to the poor by cutting at the root the two-tiered spirituality that reserves special zones for the priests and religious that are forbidden to the laity since, as there is no dividing line between the secular and the spiritual sphere.[1] It causes the total transformation of the Dalits into ONE people of God with an identity of God's people.

The Church is called to rethink its mission in the context of the community of the Dalits and to reformulate its message in order to make it relevant and meaningful to the Dalits. Developing and contextualising Dalit Theology should

---

[1] J. Neunner, S. J., "The Priest's Role in the Quest for a New Society," in *Vidyajyoti Journal of Theological Reflection*, XLVI (Delhi: Jan-Dec., 1982), p. 28.

unequivocally uphold the primacy and authority of the Scripture and root itself in a life of obedience to the Word of God and submission to the lordship of Jesus Christ. Such theological task must be done under the constant operation of the Holy Spirit with adequate hermeneutical tools and a keen awareness of God's continuing activity in Dalit history.

Bibliography

Amalorpavadass, D. S. *Theology of Evangelisation in the Indian Context*. Bangalore: National Biblical Catechetical and Liturgical Centre, 1973.

Ambedkar, Balasaheb, T H P. *Writings and Speeches*, Vol. 5. n.p.

Ariarahagm, Wesley, *Gospel and Culture: An Ongoing Discussion within the Ecumenical Movement, Gospel and Cultures Pamphlets*. Geneva: WCC, 1994.

Aruldoss, T. *Why Dalit Theology?*. Madurai: J & D Publications, 1997.

Campbell, William, *British India in its Relations to the Decline of Hindooism and the progress of Christianity*. London: n.p., 1839.

Chentharassery, *Ambedkar on Indian History*, n.p..

Choan-seng, Song, *Third-eye Theology. Theology in Formation in Asian Settings*. New York: Orbis Books, 1979.

...................., *The Compassionate God. An Exercise in the Theology of Transposition*. New York: Orbis Books, 1982.

.................., *Christian Mission in Reconstruction – An Asian Attempt*. Madras: CLS, 1975.

Coke, Burneli Arthur, (Tr.) *The Orindances of Manu*. New Delhi: n.p. 1971.

David Onesimu, J.A. *Dr. Ambedkar's Critique Towards Christian Dalit Liberation.*

Delhi: ISPCK, 2008.

Devasahaym, V. *Frontiers of Dalit Theology*. Madras: Gurukul, 1997.

Etukuri, Michael, *Toward an Indian Christian Theology*. Secunderabad: Amouthavani,

Gandhi, M.K. *Christian Missions: Their Place in India*. Ahmedabad: n.p. 1941.

Hjejile, Benedicte, *Slavery and Agricultural Bondage in South India in the Nineteenth Century*, Copenhagen, n.p. 1994.

Houghton, Graham, *The Impoverishment of Dependency*. Madras: CLS, 1983.

Fabella, Virginia, (ed.), *Asia's Struggle for Full Humanity*. Orbis Books, 1980.

Gnanakan, Ken, *Bible Theology in Asia*. Bangalore: Theological Book Trust, 1995.

Harkness, G.E. *Understanding the Kingdom of God*. New York: Abingdon, 1974.

Kananaikil, Jose, *Scheduled Castes in Search of Justice*. New Delhi: Indian Social Institute, 1986.

Kaufman, Gordon D. *In Face of Mystery: A Cognitive Theology*. Cambridge: Harvard University Press, 1993.

Keer, Dhananjay, *Dr. Ambedkar Life and Mission*. Bombay: Popular Prakashan, 1994.

Khan, Sadruddin Aga, and Hassan Bin Total, *Indigenous Peoples*. London: Zed Books Ltd., 1977.

Koyama, Kosuke, *No Handle on the Cross*. London: SCM, 1977.

Macquarrie, John, *Principles of Christian Theology*, 2nd edn. London: SCM, 1966.

Manickam, S. *Studies in Missionary History – Reflections on a Culture-Contact*. Chennai: CLS, 1988.

Massey, James, *Roots of Dalit History, Christianity, Theology and Spirituality*. Delhi: ISPCK, 1996.

Mesa Jose de, and L. Wostyn, *Doing Theology; Basic Realities and Process*. Manila: Maryhill School of Theology, 1982.

Philip, T.M. *The Encounter between Theology and Ideology*. Madras:CLS, 1986.

Pitman, G.P. *Village India*. London: Marshal, 1951.

Potts, Daniel, *British Baptist Missionaries in India*. Cambridge: Friend Of India, 1967.

Radhakrishnan, S. *Indian Philosophy*, vol. 1. n.p.

Raj, M.C. & Jyothi Raj, *Dalitology*. Bangalore: NESA, 2001.

Rajasekaran, V.C. *Reflections on Indian Christian Theology.* Madras: CLS, 1993.

Stott, John, *The Contemporary Christian.* Leicester: Inter-varsity Press, 1992.

Tamez, Elsa, *Bible of the Oppressed.* Maryknool: Orbis Press, 1982.

Thielicke, Helmut, *How Modern should Theology be,* trans. H. George Anderson. Philadelphia: Fortress Press, 1969.

Thomas, M.M. *Response to Tyranny.* New Delhi: Forum for Christian Concern for People's Struggle, 1979.

…………….. *The Christian Response to the Asian Revolution.* London: SCM, 1966.

…..……… *The Acknowledged Christ of the Indian Renaissance.* Madras: CLS, 1970.

Tiwari, Ravi, *Reflections and Studies in Religion.* Delhi: ISPCK, 2008.

Vos, Geerhardus, *Biblical Theology.* Grand Rapids: Eerdmans, 1948.

Waskom, Picket J. *Christian Mass Movements in India.* New York: Abingdon, 1933.

Webster, John, C. B. *The Dalit Christians: A History.* Delhi, ISPCK, 1992.

Wilson, K. *The Twice Alienated: Culture of Dalit Christians.* Hyderabad: Booklinks Corporation, 1982.

Yung, Hwa, *Mangoes or Bananas? The Quest for an Authentic Asian Christian Theology.* New Delhi: Oxford, 2000.

Articles in Books

Ambedkar, B.R. Philosophy and Hinduism in Vasant Moon (ed.), *Dr. Ambedkar: Writing and Speeches,* Vol. 3. Bombay: Government of Maharashtra, 1987.

Appavoo, James Theophilius "Dalit Religion," in Jams Massey (ed.) *Indigenous People: Dalits – Dalit Issues in Today's Theological Debate.* Delhi: ISPCK, 1994.

…………… *"Christology in Dalit Perspective,"* in V. Devasahayam (ed.).

Prabahkar, M.E. *"Christology in Dalit Perspective,"* in V. Devasahayam (ed.), .

Ayoorkuzhiel, A.M. Abraham "Dalit Theology: A Movement of Counter-Culture," in James Massey (ed.), *Indigenous People: Dalits – Dalit Issues in Today's Theological Debate*. Delhi: ISPCK, 1994.

Azariah, M. "Doing Theology in India Today," in R.S. Sugirtharajah & Cecil Hargreaves (eds.), *Readings in Indian Christian Theology*. Delhi: ISPCK, 1995.

Balasundaram, Franklyin J. "Dalit Theology and other Theologies," in V. Devasahayam (ed.), *Frontiers of Dalit Theology*. Delhi: ISPCK: 1997.

Bary, W. Theodore de (ed.), Excerpts in *Sources of Indian Tradition*. Delhi 1963.

Carr, Dhyanchand, "A Biblical Basis for Dalit Theology," in James Massey (ed.), *Indigenous People: Dalits – Dalit Issues in Today's Theological Debate*. Delhi: ISPCK, 1994.

Chatterji, Saral K. quoted in K. P. Kuruvila *"Dalit Theology: An Indian Christian Attempt to Give Voice to the Voiceless"* Choo, Chai-Yong, "A Brief Sketch of Korean Christian History from Minjung Perspective, in Kim Yong Bock (ed.), *In Minjung Theology. People as the subjects of History*. Singapore: Common on Theological Concerns, 1981.

Cone, James H. "The Social Context of Theology" in Choan Seng Song (ed.), *Doing Theology Today*. Madras: CLIS, 1976.

Das, Bhagwan, "Dalits and the Caste System," in Jams Massey (ed.) *Indigenous People: Dalits – Dalit Issues in Today's Theological Debate*. Delhi: ISPCK, 1994.

Devasahayam, V. "Doing Dalit Theology: Basic Assumptions," in V. Devasahayam (ed.), *Frontiers of Dalit Theology*. Delhi: ISPCK, 1997.

George, Koonthanam, *"Yahweh the Defender of the Dalits: A Reflection on Isaiah 3:12-15"*.

Koonthanam, George, "Yahweh the Defender of the Dalits: A Reflection on Isaiah 3:12- 15," in R.S. Sugirtharaj (ed.) Asian *Faces of Jesus*. New York:Orbis Books, 1993.

Koyama, Kosuke, "The Crucified Christ Challenges Human Power,' in R.S. Sugirtharaj (ed.) Asian *Faces of Jesus*. New York: Orbis Books, 1993.

Labayen, Julio, "Asian Suffering and the Christian Hope", in T.K. Thomas (ed.), *Testimony Amid Suffering*. Singapore: CCA, 1977.

Madtha, William, "Dalit Theology - Voice of the Oppressed," in James Massey (ed.), *Indigenous People: Dalits – Dalit Issues in Today's Theological Debate*. Delhi: ISPCK, 1994.

Manorama, Ruth, "Dalit Women: Downtrodden among the Downtrodden," in Jams

Massey (ed.) *Indigenous People: Dalits – Dalit Issues in Today's Theological Debate*. Delhi: ISPCK, 1994.

Minz, Nirmal, "Dalit-Tribal: A Search for Common Ideology" in James Massey (ed.), *Indigenous People*. Delhi: ISPCK, 1994.

Massey, James, "Historical Roots," in Jams Massey (ed.) *Indigenous People: Dalits – Dalit Issues in Today's Theological Debate*. Delhi: ISPCK, 1994.

.................., *"Ingredients for a Dalit Theology"*, in R.S. Sugirtharajah & Cecil Hargreaves (eds.), *Readings in Indian Christian Theology*. Delhi: ISPCK, 1995.

.................., *"A Review of Dalit Theology"*, in Samson Prabahakar and Jinkwan Kwon (eds.) *Dalit and Minjung Theologies - A Dialogue*. Bangalore: BTESSC/SATHRI, 2006.

Murray, John, "Systematic Theology," in *The Collected Writings of John Murray*, Vol. 4. Edinburgh: Banner of Truth Trust, 1982.

N.P. Williams, "What is Theology?" in Kenneth E. Erik (ed.) *The Study of Theology*. London, n.p.

Nirmal, Arvind, "Towards a Christian Theology" in M.E. Prabhakar (ed.), *Towards a Dalit Theology*. Delhi: ISPCK, 1988.

Prabahkar, M.E. "Christology in Dalit Perspective," in V. Devasahayam (ed.), *Frontiers of Dalit Theology*. Delhi: ISPCK, 1997.

.... "The Search for a Dalit Theology," in James Massey (ed.), *Indigenous People: Dalits – Dalit Issues in Today's Theological Debate*. Delhi: ISPCK, 1994.

Pawde, Kumud, "The Position of Dalit Women in Indian Society," in Jams Massey (ed.) *Indigenous People: Dalits – Dalit Issues in Today's Theological Debate*. Delhi: ISPCK, 1994.

Razu, John Mohan, "Contours and Trajectories of Dalit Theology", in Samson

Prabahakar and Jinkwan Kwon (eds.) *Dalit and Minjung Theologies - A Dialogue.* Bangalore: BTESSC/SATHRI, 2006.

Shiri, Godwin, "Glimpses from the 19th century – Missionary Crusade Against Caste: Lessons for Doing Theology Today", in Samson Prabahakar and Jinkwan Kwon (eds.) *Dalit and Minjung Theologies - A Dialogue.* Bangalore: BTESSC/ SATHRI, 2006.

Singh, Kapur, "Mohenjodaro" in *Pundreek.* Ambala: n.p., 1952.

Suh, David Kwang-Sun, "A Biographic Sketch of an Asian Theological Consultation," in Kim Yong Bock (ed.), *In Minjung Theology. People as the subjects of History.* Singapore: Common on Theological Concerns, 1981.

Wan, Enoch, "Critiquing the Method of Traditional Western Theology and Calling for Sino-Theology," 1998.

Wheeler, Sir Mortiner, "The Cambridge History of India, Supplementary Volume," in *The Indus Civilization.* Cambridge: n.p.1953.

Wolf, C.U. "Poor" in *Interpreter's Dictionary of the Bible.* New York: Abingdon Press, 1962.

Articles in Periodicals

Abraham, K.C. "Emerging Concerns in Third World Theology", *Bangalore Theological Forum* Vol. XXVI, No.3 & 4. Sept and Dec, 1994.

.... "Third World Theologies", *CTC Bulletin*, May-December 1992.

Amebdkar, "Philosophy of Hinduism," in *Writings and Speeches*, Vol. iii.

Balasuriya, Tissa, "Theologizing from the Other Side of the World", *Logos*, Vol. 20, No. 3, Sept. 1981.

Blaesch, Donald, G. "The Renewal of Theology" *Evangelical Review of Theology* 23/2 1992.

Blundell, David, "Eternal Fighter" India Today, Vol. XXXIII No. 16 April 15-21 2008.

Carino, Feliciano, "What About the Theology of Struggle?" in *Religion and Society*, Manila: FIDES, 1988.

Emmanuel, Justine, "Living with Ignominy," *Indian Currents*, Vol. XX, No. 13-14   2008.

Gaffin, Richard, "Systematic and Biblical Theology," *Westminster Theological Journal* 38. 1975-76.

Gnanavaram, M. "Eschatology in Dalit Perspective," in V D (ed.), FODT.

Hyun, Young-Hak, "Minjung Theology and the Religion of Han," East Asia Journal Theology, 3.2. 1985.

Jha, Vivekanand, "Stages in History of Untouchables, *The Indian Historical Review II*, July 1975.

Kalliath Antony, "Revisiting Liberation Theology in a Neo-Liberal World I," *Vidyahyoti Journal of Theological Reflection*, Vol. 72, No. 3, March 2008.

Kani, Jacob, "Editor's Message" *Indian Currents*, Vol. XX, No. 13-14   2008.

Kim, Heup Young, "A Tao way of Asian Theology in the 21st century: From the perspective of the Ugmchi Phenomen," in Renthy Keitzar (ed.), Journal of Tribal Studies, Vol. IV, No. 2, July-December, 2000.

Kuruvila "Dalit Theology: An Indian Christian Attempt to Give Voice to the Voiceless."

Massey, James A. "Scheduled Caste: A Special Reference to Scheduled Caste Origin", *Religion and Society* Vol. XXXXVIII, No.3. March, 1991.

M.M. Thomas, "The Christological Task in India" *Religion and Society* (Sep. 1964), p. 1.

Moore, Michael S. "A Critical Profile of Choan-Seng Song's Theology." *Missiology* 10:4 1982.

Musafir, Subhas Chandra, "A Section of Educated Dalits have Become Mini-Brahmins", *Dalit Voice*, July 15-31, 1999.

Neunner, J. "The Priest's Role in the Quest for a New Society," in *Vidyajyoti Journal of Theological Reflection*, XLVI. Delhi: Jan-Dec., 1982.

Paul II, Pope John. quoted by Justine Emmanuel, "Living with Ignominy," *Indian Currents*, Vol. XX, No. 13-14 2008.

Pinto, Ambrose, "Kanshi Ram: A Challenge to NGOs" *Indian Currents*, 30 Oct,-Nov. 2006.

Putra, Bharat, "The Great Conversion," *Indian Currents*, 16-22 October 2006.

................., "Judgment Reserved", Indian Currents, 30 Oct,-Nov. 2006.

Rajagopal, P. "Caste in its Relation to the Church", *Indian Evangelical Review*, vol. IV, January 1877.

Ramaiah, A. "The Dalit Issue: A Hindu Perspective," in Jams Massey (ed.) *Indigenous People: Dalits – Dalit Issues in Today's Theological Debate*. Delhi: ISPCK, 1994.

Savariaradimai, Emanuel, "Caste Ghost Haunts Church," *Indian Currents*, Vol. XX, No. 13-14 2008.

Se-yoon, Kim, "Is "Minjung Theology" a Christian Theology?" Calvin Theology Journal. 22:2. 1987.

Simbo, Billy K. "An African Critique of Western Theology," *Evangelical Review of Theology* Vol. 7, Number 1, April 1983.

Song, Choan-seng, "New China and Salvation History – A Methodological Inquiry," *S.E. Asia Journal of Theology*, 15:2. 1974.

Reports and Newspaper Articles

BBC News Article: *Low-caste Hindus adopt new faith*, Last accessed 15 October 2006 Bombay Harijans Resolution, October 17, 1945.

Government of India, *National Census of India 2001*, Final Population Totals, 2004.

Grey, Mary, "Dalit Women and the Struggle for Justice in a World of Global Capitalism" in Ranjita Biswas, Society: On the Wings of Dreams, The Hindu, May 13, 2007.

Karthikeyan, K."Electrified wall divides people on caste lines" *The Hindu*, April 17, 2008.

................., "The dividing wall remains but loses its electric string" *The Hindu*, April 18, 2008.

Report of the Backward Classes Commission, Government of India, First Part, Vol. I & II, 1980.

Report in the *Bulletin of the Institute of Traditional Cultures*, Madras University, 1980.

Report of the Board of Education for the year 1840-1841.

Report of Prevention of Atrocities against SCs and STs, *National Human Rights Commission*, New Delhi, 2004.

Report of Group II in Social Action Groups and the Churches in India – A Consultation, Bangalore, CISRS, 1984.

L.M. Shrikant, "Report of the Commissioner for Scheduled Castes and Scheduled Tribes for the period ending 31st December 1951.

Ram Vilas Paswan, "Dalit Forum", *The Hindu*, December 28, 2007, p. 13.

Saheli, "Dalit Women and the Struggle for Justice in a World of Global Capitalism" in Ranjita Biswas, Society: On the Wings of Dreams, The Hindu, May 13, 2007.

Special Correspondent, "Untouchability Prevails", *The Hindu*, December 28, 2007, p. 7.

Thonthi, Marimuthu, "Electrified wall divides people on caste lines" *The Hindu*, April 17, 2008.

Internet Sources

Aristide, Jean-Bertrand, "Liberation Theology" at http://mb-soft.com/ believe/ txn/ liberati.html

http://en.wikipedia.org/wiki/Dalit

Gutierrez, Gustavo, "A Theology of Liberation" quoted by Jean-Bertrand Aristide, "Liberation Theology" at http://mb-soft.com/believe/txn/liberati.htm

Knapp, Stephen, "Casteism: Is It the Scourge of Hinduism, or the Perversion of a Legitimate Vedic System?" http://www.stephen-knapp.com

Kuruvila K. P. "Dalit Theology: An Indian Christian Attempt to Give Voice to the Voiceless."

Mathew, C. V. "Contextual Theology", http://www.nathaniel.turner.com/ contextualtheology.htm

Prasad, Chandra Bhan, "Democracy a form of society or a form of governance" New Delhi: Dalit Shiksha Andolan, 2008. www.dalitchristians.com/Html/survey.htm

Richard, "Liberation Theology in the New International Context - New Themes and Challenges" http://mb-soft.com/believe/txn/liberati.htm

Sobrino, Juan, quoted by Jean-Bertrand Aristide, "Liberation Theology" in http://mb-soft.com/ believe/txn/liberati.htm

The Seventh NCSC/ST Report (2001-2002). http://en.wikipedia.org/wiki/Dalit

Webster, D. D. Elwell Evangelical Dictionary, quoted in Jean-Bertrand Aristide,

"Liberation Theology" at http://mb-soft.com/believe/txn/liberati.htm

www.dalitchristians.com/Html/survey.htm